The Shareholder Action Handbook

Using Shares to make Companies more Accountable

Craig Mackenzie

A New Consumer Guide

For Roddy and Sylvia Mackenzie,
without whom . . .

First published in Great Britain in 1993
by New Consumer Ltd,
52 Elswick Road, Newcastle upon Tyne NE4 6JH

ISBN 1 897806 00 0

Typeset in Caslon 224 by Bookcraft, Stroud, Gloucestershire
Printed by Biddles Ltd, Guildford, Surrey

Contents

PART ONE:
THE NATURE OF COMPANIES

PART TWO:
SHAREHOLDER ACTION

Acknowledgements

This book would not have been written without the generous support of two institutions. Firstly, I am most grateful for the wide-ranging help provided by New Consumer and its staff. I am particularly indebted to Richard Adams, its director, whose advice and hard work have been vital to the book's appearance in print. Secondly, I acknowledge with gratitude grant support from the Joseph Rowntree Charitable Trust.

Many of the organisations mentioned in the following pages have proved to be invaluable sources of detailed information about the practice of Shareholder Action, for which considerable thanks are due. Particular mention is owed to Stuart Bell of PIRC Ltd, Mark Campanale of Jupiter Tyndall Merlin, Dave Craine of ELTSA, and Mark Hayes of Shared Interest, who gave not only valuable advice, but also critical comments on sections of the book, to its considerable benefit. I am also grateful to Roger Moody and PARTiZANS who allowed be to observe their shareholder action surrounding the 1992 AGM of The RTZ Corporation PLC.

Any errors of fact or interpretation in the text are the author's responsibility. It should be particularly noted that the author is not a trained lawyer, so the many references to points of law made in the book should be understood as a lay person's interpretation, not professional legal advice.

The book attempts to use 'inclusive' language with one notable exception: while the directors of big companies are both men and women (though mainly men), the chair-people of these companies remain exclusively chair*men*. This is reflected in the text.

What is New Consumer?

New Consumer is a charitable public interest research organisation. It publishes information about the social, environmental and ethical performance and policy of companies. New Consumer's research is used by the press, by campaigning groups, and by companies themselves. New Consumer is supported by major charitable trusts, educational establishments, international development agencies and by the European Commission. New Consumer does not accept sponsorship from or on behalf of corporations or organisations.

New Consumer's current publications list includes:

Changing Corporate Values Kogan Page, April 1991, £48 Hardback, £19.95 paper, 637pp. Rated as 'a groundbreaking book in British Business Ethics', it examines the social, environmental and ethical performance of 128 major consumer market companies in the UK. It is the definitive introduction to the assessment of corporate responsibility issues.

Shopping for a Better World Kogan Page, September 1991, £4.99, 288pp. A pocket guide to socially responsible shopping, rating the companies behind over 2,500 popular brand names. It provides a sketch of corporate policies as well as an effective guide to who owns which brands.

The Global Consumer Victor Gollancz, October 1991, £5.95, 340pp, looks at how our everyday purchases help or hinder the third world. It enables consumers to mobilise their spending power in a way that is constructive to the development process.

Britain's Best Employers? Kogan Page, November 1992, £10.95, 340pp, is the first book to provide job hunters with impartial advice and information across the entire range of the business, social and ethical activities of the country's major graduate employers, both public and private sector.

New Consumer undertakes a range of research and advisory work on issues of corporate responsibility, sustainable development, the social market and social entrepreneurship. All the above publications are available (post free) together with more information from New Consumer 52 Elswick Road Newcastle upon Tyne NE4 6JH; Tel 091 272 1148.

Introduction

Large companies are among the most potent economic and social forces in the modern world. The actions they take have important consequences for the rest of society. For example, common company policy decisions include:

- The location, relocation and closure of company factories and offices
- Investment in new technologies
- The environmental impact of production processes, and the disposal of toxic waste
- The equality of employment opportunities for members of disadvantaged groups
- The management of trade relationships with third world suppliers
- The sale of weapons to controversial foreign governments
- The financial support by companies of political parties

Each of these company policy decisions affects society as a whole, and yet it is frequently the case that those affected most by company decisions, those with the most to lose, are excluded from the decision-making processes. This book provides a practical guide for people who wish to include themselves in the corporate policy-making process.

In British law companies are largely self-regulating institutions. The primary structure of self-regulation is the shareholder system. In theory, under this system the shareholders appoint company directors and hold them accountable for their actions. The shareholders entrust the directors with day-to-day control over the company, the directors in consequence have the legal obligation to act in good faith on the shareholders' behalf. While, in practice, the shareholder system has significant problems, it remains the case that the system does give shareholders considerable potential power in companies. Consequently, one of the best ways for people to ensure that their interests are represented in the corporate decision-making process is for them to buy shares and use them to take shareholder action.

Shareholder action is a loose term to describe the attempt to influence corporate decision-making through the shareholder process. This wide definition encompasses action by individuals, small campaigning groups, large national pressure groups, and institutional investors like pension funds. While mainstream shareholder concerns — like the level of shareholders' dividend payments — fall within the above definition, for the purposes of this book, shareholder action refers particularly to a range of social and ethical corporate policy questions. Shareholder action in the pursuit of social interests has become increasingly common in the last two decades, particularly in the United States. In 1992 several hundred companies faced socially motivated shareholder action campaigns. The overwhelming majority of these campaigns took place in America, but in recent years a growing number of British companies have faced pressure from shareholder activists on social issues. The concerns shareholder activists have pursued include: company investment policies in South Africa and Northern Ireland; the production of military hardware and arms sales to controversial foreign governments; environmental policy; equal opportunities policy; and corporate trading relationships with third world countries. There have been a few shareholder actions by conservative political groups, but the overwhelming majority of shareholder action continues to represent progressive, liberal social interests.

Shareholder activists have few realistic hopes of forcing changes in company policy directly by, say, out-voting the board of directors at a shareholders' meeting. Instead shareholder activists have used the media, institutional investors, regulators, and legislators to put pressure on companies to make concrete corporate policy improvements. Where shareholder activists have been successful, especially in America, they have secured a range of other objectives including the emergence of a more sensitive and self-conscious business community, and the mobilisation of sections of the politically central, shareholding middle classes.

In Britain there are now around ten million individual private shareholders. Most of these are small-scale investors who bought their shares during the recent waves of government privatisation of public utilities and industries. In addition to this direct share ownership, most adults in this country have a substantial indirect interest in company shares; either through their pension plans, or through other institutions in which they have an interest — such as their insurance company, local authority, church or trade union. Direct and indirect share ownership provides the public with considerable opportunities for influencing company policy. This handbook provides the information necessary to make use of these opportunities.

The book is in two parts. Many readers may prefer to start with the second part, which concerns the more practical side of shareholder action; providing the reader with the detailed information and suggestions about how to plan and take shareholder action. Part One looks at the history and theory of shareholders and companies, and examines the need for a change in the structure of the shareholder process.

No specialist knowledge of business, finance, law or share ownership is necessary to make use of this book. It is aimed at the lay person. While the examples the book uses to illustrate shareholder action largely concern action by groups pursuing social or environmental agendas, shareholder action can be used for a very broad range of purposes. Whatever the purpose, this book hopes to show how members of the public can, over a period of time, bring decisive influence to bear on the policies of companies, by taking intelligent, carefully planned action using shares.

Part One
The Nature
of Companies

Chapter 1
The History of the Company

Companies are often thought of in economic terms, as the institutions that manufacture products, provide services and employ people. But, for the purposes of shareholder action, it is at least as important to think about companies as legal institutions, as it is to think about them as economic ones. The law affects most aspects of company behaviour: it provides the regulatory environment in which companies operate (product safety standards, for example); it defines the boundary between free enterprise and fraud; and it sets out how much tax companies must pay. In this respect the law for companies is similar to the law for people; it says what they can and cannot do. But for companies the law does more than this. Companies, unlike people, owe their very existence to the law. The law defines who owns and controls companies, and it defines what rights and responsibilities these controllers should have. According to company law, companies are independent entities which have a similar legal status to people — like people they can, for example, own things and sue for damages. This status, and the legal privileges associated with it, has contributed very strongly to the success of modern economies. The details of the legal position of companies will be discussed in the following chapters. The rest of this chapter examines the evolution of their legal status.

The Guilds

The word company, like the word companion, derives from the Latin *com* — with, *panis* — bread, and so means 'people sharing bread together'. This serves as a reminder that companies originated as groups of people associating together and sharing resources in order to pursue a common purpose. The first businesses associations in Britain were the craft and merchant guilds of the middle ages. Before the guilds, individuals had tended to do business alone. Guilds became common from the twelfth century onwards. The guilds were initially small, relatively local associations formed by local crafts and tradespeople (the fishmongers, the saddlers, the weavers, the grocers and the goldsmiths). The guilds regulated trade in the local market over which the members of the guild held a monopoly. They behaved in similar ways to the professional organisations that exist today, like the British Medical Association or the Institution of Civil Engineers, for example. The guilds both protected and regulated their members. They set the qualifications that were required for guild membership; they ensured that product quality reached a certain standard; and they controlled competition by limiting the hours individual guild members were allowed to work. The guilds started off as small, weak organisations, but evolved into rich and powerful institutions. Many of them still exist as the livery companies of London, although they are no longer very influential.

The guilds employed quite different business practices from those used by modern companies. While the guilds, like modern companies, could be described as 'people associating together in order to pursue a particular shared purpose,' they were only very loose associations. Individual guild members traded on their own behalf, taking the risks and receiving the rewards of business themselves. Individual businesses were owned and controlled by the tradespeople who managed them, not by the guild association as a whole. Large modern companies, on the other hand, trade as associations, not as individual tradespeople. One of the reasons for the difference is the dramatically different moral codes existing in the past. The moral attitude in Britain during the middle ages, which persisted at least until the last century, despised cut-throat competition and undeserved personal profit. While it was thought tolerable for craftspeople or merchants to earn an 'honest living' from selling the goods they had made or transported, it was not considered acceptable for people to profit undeservedly from the work of others. One prominent historian described this as 'the unpardonable sin of the speculator or middleman who snatches private gain by the exploitation of public necessities'.[1] Undeserved personal profit was an evil, of the same kind as usury. Individuals were expected to earn their money through their own labours, not vicariously through the work of others. Consequently the law prohibited people from making money without earning it for themselves. This approach would effectively have disallowed most of the business arrangements of the modern world. Sleeping partners, shareholders and banks who gain profit from simply lending money, would have been seen as wicked profiteers and usurers.

Since the middle ages, speculation and profit-making have slowly become respectable, to the extent that these activities are today becoming public virtues. People who excel at making profits without having worked terribly hard for them are now, for some people, modern heroes. The large scale sell-off of public utilities at bargain prices has contributed to making speculation a common pursuit, although, in these days of recession and city scandal, the gloss applied to these activities during the 'Lawson boom' has become tarnished.

Partnerships and Chartered Companies

The change in the moral status of profit and speculation has been evolutionary rather than revolutionary. In Britain, as early as the sixteenth century, the requirement for individuals to earn profits exclusively from their own labours relaxed, and it became common for individuals to trade together, profiting from each other's work.

The first legal forms of business which allowed 'unearned' profits were known as *societas* and *commenda*. The *commenda* commonly allowed a sleeping partnership, where one person provided the money and the other their time and business skills. Both shared in the profits of the enterprise, and the risk of the sleeping partner was limited to the initial capital invested. This arrangement was like a loan, but instead of interest, which was considered morally dubious, the lender took a share in the profits. The *commenda* never became widely popular in Britain, although it has traditionally been a major form of business arrangement in the rest of Europe. The *societas* was the forerunner of modern partnerships: under this form of organisation each partner is considered the agent of all the others, each is liable for the others' debts, and all the risks and all the rewards were shared.

During the same period another form of legal structure emerged for larger scale trading enterprises: the chartered corporation. Chartered companies were formed, by Royal Charter or under an Act of Parliament. The process of the formation of these companies, or 'corporate bodies', became known as 'incorporation'. The term is still in use today — US companies have to put Inc. (short for incorporated) after their name. The first people to use this new legal form of business were the merchant adventurers such as the East India Company. These companies were in some respects international versions of guilds. They were genuine 'associations of people gathered for a shared purpose' — authentic 'companies' of merchants. The members of chartered corporations traded with their own goods and their own money, the company only provided a framework for collective action — like the hiring of ships and the building of warehouses — and provided rules and regulations to keep trading fair. Chartered status was useful because it allowed companies a monopoly, as well as governmental authority, over British trading outposts overseas, conferring on the members of these incorporated companies considerable legally enshrined benefits and powers.[2] The Crown also benefited from its creation of these chartered companies by gaining control over British trade, and over the overseas operations of the chartered companies.

While initially the members of chartered corporations traded individually with their own goods, during the seventeenth century it became common for members of the company to pool the goods they were trading. These goods were known as their 'stock', so these companies were known as 'joint stock' companies. (This is confusing because 'stock', as in 'stocks and shares', also means the capital of a company, that is to say the store of money used for carrying out business. Individuals in joint stock companies pooled their goods, not their money.) The East India Company, The Muscovy Company, The Virginia Company, and the North West Passage Company were examples of joint stock trading companies. In the East India Company, formed in 1600, individual trading with joint stock became common by 1653, and in 1692 the old form of individual trading was no longer allowed.[3] Joint stock trading allowed the risk and the profit of trading to be shared in proportion to an individual's investment.

The Emergence of Limited Liability

While chartered or incorporated companies became common, in the eighteenth century the bulk of trading was still by sole proprietors and small partnerships. These businesses were completely financed from the funds of the entrepreneurs themselves. This meant that these businesses were regularly short of money for investment, thus limiting growth. To meet this shortage of funds, many entrepreneurs turned to relatively wealthy individuals who wished to secure a good return on their surplus wealth. These individuals bought shares and became sleeping partners or investors in the firm. From the investors point of view, however, these arrangements had one drawback — it was common for both partners to be jointly liable for the partnership's debts. Thus sleeping partners could not afford to sleep too deeply. The requirement for investors to share the risks associated with the business was uncomfortable and discouraging for them. But that was the point. Making profits from one's money at no personal cost was precisely the kind of thing that was abhorred by the premodern moral order. The discomfort of risk was the price that investors had to pay for earning money without working for it. Despite the burden of risk, these 'unincorporated' partnerships became quite common.

By the end of the seventeenth century, a distinction began to be drawn between a company's acts and those of its members; between the actions taken under the name of the formal business association and the actions of people participating in it. The formal company entity could, for the first time, own property and sue on its own behalf. Previously, only the members of the company could do these things, on behalf of their association. Another advantage of the emerging distinction between a company and its members was that companies could exist indefinitely, even if their founders died. This allowed the accumulated wealth and trading connections of companies to be passed on, without having to be recreated every generation. The appropriation of independent legal status by companies meant that companies became liable for their own debts. This was taken to imply that, if the company was liable for its debts, then the members of the company could not also be liable. Consequently, for the first time, investors of capital could, in theory, use the corporate body as protection against financial risk, 'limiting' their 'liability'. Under this principle, if a company went broke, creditors would have to sue the company entity and not its members. In practice, however, this did not work. If a company needed money to repay its debts, its directors were able, on behalf of the company, to call in extra money from the members; and, in any case, creditors found ways of suing the members directly.

However, the idea that the company could limit the potential liability its members faced in a case of bankruptcy, say, proved to be an attractive one.

Previously, in accordance with the prevailing moral principles, all those people holding a share of a company faced unlimited, joint liability for any losses the firm might make. This applied to unincorporated businesses and incorporated ones alike. Unlimited liability meant that if a company collapsed, owing large sums of money to creditors, the members of the company were liable for every penny. It meant that the failure of a business could bankrupt anyone who held shares in it. This usually meant the owners, their families, and any friends who had helped out. For example, in 1809 Sir Walter Scott, the novelist, had invested some money in his publisher, Ballantyne. The company subsequently went bankrupt. Together with the other investors, he was personally obliged to pay off the company's huge debt. He did so by writing, prolifically, the large number of novels that he is now famous for.[4]

Although perhaps fortunate for English literature, unlimited liability, to twentieth century eyes, might seem a dangerous way to carry out business. In eighteenth century Britain, however, unlimited liability was considered the only straight and morally responsible way to do business. Furthermore, it was believed that the public interest would be endangered if businessmen were able to undertake hazardous endeavours at no personal risk to themselves. Limiting liability, it was felt, would provide a charter for the foolish, the irresponsible and the dishonest to carry out highly speculative ventures, heedless of the consequences to others.

The South Sea Bubble

Unlimited liability, however, was not a failsafe way of protecting the public. Unscrupulous people found it quite possible to undertake extremely risky ventures, funded by a credulous public. In the early eighteenth century, many investors lost large sums of money in a number of chancy business that collapsed. This has come to be known as the period of the 'bubbles', most notably the South Sea Bubble. The bubbles were companies with unsustainably inflated share prices. Prices pumped up by misleading claims about the security and profitability of the investments, and escalated further by unreasonably bullish overconfidence. The fact that shares in these companies were easily transferable enabled speculators to jump on the bandwagon, driving the value of the shares higher. Investors unwittingly exposed themselves to huge liabilities with little prospect of gain.

Many of the companies experiencing bubbles on their stock were unincorporated companies passing themselves off as incorporated ones, or chartered companies involved in businesses quite different from those for which their charter was originally intended. This was exacerbated because charters of companies were regularly traded. For example a bank purchased the charter of the Sword Blade Company, which had unsurprisingly made sword blades before closing down. The bank then used this charter from a manufacturing company as the regulatory basis for its banking business. This kind of abuse was dangerous because chartered companies, while operating under the purposes for which they were incorporated, were to some extent regulated, by their own rules and by Parliament, but companies misusing their charter were largely unregulated. In 1720 there was enough concern about the highly risky and speculative nature of many of these dubious companies for Parliament to introduce the Bubble Act to attempt to prevent this kind of abuse of chartered status. It also aimed to curb the growth of unincorporated joint stock companies, which were at the time virtually unregulated. The Bubble Act was vague and incoherent, but it did question the status of a range of speculative companies. When prosecutions of these companies were first made under the Act, full-scale panic ensued and many of the bubbles burst. The South Sea Company was the most famous of these. It had been engaged on an extraordinary scheme to buy the whole of the national debt by buying out the current holders. The company thought that owning control of a country's debt would provide excellent collateral for raising money for itself (countries are not supposed to be able to go bankrupt, so holding the national debt was considered to be a secure asset). The scheme proved too expensive for the company, however, and after the Bubble Act the shares of the South Sea Company fell by 90%. Many other companies collapsed completely. Consequently, chartered joint stock companies became unpopular for the next hundred years.

It is ironic that the Bubble Act was supposed to protect investors against loss arising from the collapse of dubious and speculative companies, and yet its introduction led to the ruin of thousands of the people it set out to safeguard. A further irony is that while the Bubble Act aimed to stop the spread of unincorporated companies, it made it so difficult to gain a charter and become incorporated that unincorporated companies became a dominant form of business by the end of the eighteenth century.

Dodging the Bubble Act

During the period following the Act, unincorporated companies found ways to trade as 'trusts', neatly side-stepping the Bubble Act. The trusts set up were regulated under deeds of settlement, which restricted the transfer of shares, and contained detailed rules about company management. The trusts were more like partnerships than incorporated companies. They could not sue under the firm's name, and if someone wanted to sue them, the partners had to be sued individually. These unincorporated trusts lacked limited liability, so all the partners were fully liable for the debts of the business. While this unlimited liability was in line with the traditional moral principles and served to protect society at large from injudicious businessmen, it also caused the old problem that business lacked the money to expand and develop because few people were prepared to risk their entire wealth on investment. With little investment capital, businesses and the economy as a whole could not grow very fast. Furthermore, they were faced with considerable legal problems in reclaiming their debts. Creditors wanting to sue a trust had to sue its individual members. Consequently, in the case of trusts, unlimited liability provided a disincentive to investors, while not providing effective protection to creditors.

The Invention of the Modern Company

The Bubble Act was finally repealed in 1825 because it was failing to achieve most of its intentions. Also in 1825, the Board of Trade took over the Crown's responsibility for chartering companies. Companies could now apply to be chartered by Letters Patent, rather than Royal Charter or Act of Parliament. In 1837, the Board of Trade was allowed to incorporate companies with limited liability. It did so rarely, and the majority of business continued to be carried out by sole traders, partnerships and unincorporated trusts. In 1843 the Board of Trade, under William Gladstone, later Prime Minister, set up a committee to look into joint stock companies.

Their report was the first serious and systematic attempt to examine company law. It provided the basis for the Joint-Stock Companies Act of 1844, which effectively invented the modern company. The three principles which it contained still remain in force today. First, it formally distinguished private partnerships from joint stock companies. The latter had to be registered. Secondly, it made incorporation still easier by allowing companies to incorporate by simply registering with the Board of Trade. Thirdly, it forced incorporated companies to account publicly for their activities. The Act required companies to have directors and a secretary; to hold regular meetings of shareholders and to appoint a chairman for these meetings; to make accounts, to have them audited by auditors, and to report the results to the shareholders.

While Gladstone's Act represented a radical reworking of company law, it did not immediately lead to a boom in the number of new companies. Part of the problem was that it still did not generally allow limited liability. While the Bill did set up an incorporated legal entity, creditors could still sue individual members of the company. In any case, incorporation was not very popular with business-people. It did not generate the businesslike, entrepreneurial impression that it does today. Corporate status in the past could only be gained by lobbying Parliament or the Crown, so it had long been associated with political influence, vested interests and monopoly power. Also, an air of moral disapproval and uncertainty hung over the idea of incorporation, which allowed people to hide behind a legal façade rather than doing business openly on their own account. Despite these concerns, over 900 companies registered over the ten years following the Act.

There was pressure on the government to go one step further and allow registered, incorporated companies to have limited liability as well. The society that campaigned for a change in the law to allow this argued that if incorporated companies were allowed limited status then 'capital . . . [could] be advanced by respectable persons . . . to answer the wants of our increasing enterprise at home and in our foreign dependencies.'[5] Limited liability finally became widely available to incorporated companies, despite much controversy over the issue, in the Limited Liability Act of 1855. Registered companies that gained limited liability had to meet certain financial requirements and had to attach the word 'Limited' to their name in order to warn the investing public of the fact. In the six years following this Act 2,479 companies were registered.

Reinventing the Company

In 1856 this bill was replaced with one that sought to consolidate all the company law that had been produced into one document. However, economic liberalism was a powerful intellectual force at the time. The dominant mood then, perhaps even more than it is today, was that government should not interfere in the market-place. Consequently, the new Act removed most of the regulatory safeguards that aimed to protect the public from the consequences of limited liability. For example, it no longer became compulsory for directors to appoint auditors to examine the company accounts. Practically the only effective provision for protecting investors was that companies still had to append the word 'Limited' to their name. The principle was that,

> those who dealt with companies knowing them to be limited had only themselves to blame if they burnt their fingers. The mystic word 'Limited' was intended to act as a red flag warning the public of the dangers which they ran if they had dealings with the dangerous new invention.[6]

However as we see today, the fact that most companies have 'Ltd.' written after their name hardly deters people from doing deals with them. We have little choice. The losses that creditors make when limited liability companies fail are now treated as a business expense, and are compensated for by creditors charging higher rates of interest on loans, the cost of which can then be passed on to consumers. So, ultimately the public end up paying much of the costs of limited liability for companies.

The 1862 Act required that for a company to be formed, seven people must subscribe their name to a Memorandum of Association. This, for limited companies, had to contain: the word 'limited' wherever the company name appeared, the address of the registered office, the objectives of the company and the capital that the company proposed to have registered. The law also declared that the company must hold a meeting every year. These company meetings are today known as annual general meetings or AGMs. The 1862 Act also empowered the Board of Trade, now the Department of Trade and Industry, to appoint inspectors to examine the affairs of the company, on application of not less than a fifth of the shareholders. The 1855 and 1862 Companies Acts made British company law the most permissive in Europe,[7] and in many ways it still remains so. Following the legislation, company registrations boomed.

By the time the 1862 Act was passed the central principles of modern company law were in place. People with spare capital could profitably invest it in companies, without having to be involved in the running of the company, and with strict limitations on the risks they faced. Companies could act in their own name, making contracts, owning property, suing and being sued. However, while the statutory structure was in position, there were a large number of questions that the statute left unanswered. These gaps have, to a large extent, subsequently been filled by the courts, which have interpreted the statutes and introduced common law presumptions into company law.

Summary of Recent History

Legislation for companies has been under periodic review by expert committees appointed by successive governments. The recommendations of these committees have to varying degrees been incorporated into updated versions of the Companies Act. The most comprehensive revisions took place in the 1948 and 1985 Companies Acts. In addition to the Companies Act and company case law, the Stock Exchange has also instituted a wide range of requirements for companies wishing to be listed by it. These are set out in the 'Yellow Book' and, in the early part of this century, were substantially more rigorous than the company law of the time.

In the nineteenth century, changes in company law aimed to make the process of incorporation cheaper and less difficult. In the twentieth century, the review committees have been more anxious to make the legal corporate structure work more efficiently. The Cohen committee, which reported prior to the 1948 Companies Act, recommended that 'as much information as is reasonably required shall be made available to the shareholders and creditors of companies and to the general public'[8] and that a way should be found for 'making it easier for shareholders to exercise a more effective general control over the management of their companies'.

These sentiments were echoed by the Jenkins Committee in the 1960s, and more recently. However, the steps taken to remedy the inadequacies of shareholder control of companies have not produced notable success, leading one of the more influential commentators on company law to conclude that,

> It seems likely that future development here will recognise that it is unreal to expect the members of large public companies to control the management and that a State agency must do so instead.[9]

Subsequent chapters will examine this view, and the many weaknesses of the law as it stands. One government minister said in the 1960s that there was an urgent need for wide 're-forms in the structure and philosophy of our company law', he also said that it was necessary to 're-examine the whole theory and purpose of the limited joint stock company, the comparative rights and obligations of shareholders, directors, creditors, employees and the community as a whole'.[10] That was 25 years ago. The re-examination has not taken place, and the need is now perhaps greater than it was then. The next chapter lays out the form of company law as it now stands. Following it is a discussion of what could be done to provide for better company control and accountability.

Chapter 2
Companies and the Law

The basic principles of the modern company were developed in the mid-nineteenth century. Current company law differs in detail from what it was then but, despite large changes in the way companies work, the principles remain largely unaltered. There are significant discrepancies between the way company law expects corporate governance to work and the way it actually does. This section will ignore these discrepancies and present a summary of the law as it stands. It will not attempt to cover the whole of company law. The main piece of legislation, the Companies Act (1985), runs to several hundred pages on its own, and there is much more to company law than the Companies Act. This section will cover only those sections most relevant to understanding what the company is, who controls it and what rights are available to shareholders.

Inconveniently, as for most parts of British law, there is no single, comprehensive rule book that the public may consult for a full, clear understanding of company law. Instead, because it has evolved over a long period of time, company law is a sprawling, haphazard and often inconsistent mixture of case law and government legislation, or statute law. Case law and statute law are of quite different kinds. The former is made up of rulings of individual members of the judiciary. These rulings are often inconsistent and usually highly specific to individual disputes. Understanding it therefore involves making sense of the set of circumstances relating to each case. The case law for companies goes back over 100 years, and so provides a wealth of contradictory precedents and interpretations. Statute law on the other hand is more generally applicable and consistent, though new statutes are periodically grafted onto old, overlapping without totally replacing them. A further obstacle to understanding both kinds of law is the fact that it is presented in legal jargon, which is arranged in tortuous sentences, often peppered with Latin phrases.

There are, however, a number of useful guide books (see bibliography). These tend to include a certain amount of legal jargon, but are relatively easy to follow. The following section provides a summary of the central principles of company law. It should be noted that while this summary aims to be reliable, the law is complex and subject to varying interpretations, this section should therefore be read as a rough sketch, rather than a text book exposition.

Company Law

There are numerous kinds of business enterprise: sole trader, partnership, cooperative, public corporation, and company. The Companies Acts only regulates the latter; there are other laws for other forms of enterprise. Company law provides regulations for the creation of companies; it defines their basic structure; and it regulates the relationship between companies, their directors, and their members. It does not attempt to regulate the actual day-to-day running of a business. That is not to say that the day-to-day operations go unregulated, there are a wide range of other laws which regulate business activity, including tax law, contract law, labour law, monopoly law, health and safety law, equal opportunities law, and environmental law. While there is some overlap with these other laws, company law concerns itself with defining the 'constitutional' arrangements for companies, that is to say: how they are set up and how they are closed down; how they are to be owned and how they can be bought and sold; how they are to be controlled and how the controllers are to be held accountable for their actions. For the purposes of shareholder action, those parts of company law which deal with ownership, control and accountability are of greatest relevance. This section will concentrate on them.

There are a wide variety of different types of company: public and private, limited and unlimited, for-profit and not-for-profit to name a few. This guide will deal predominantly with limited companies which may offer shares for sale to the public. This category covers almost all the biggest companies in Britain. While there are a few large private companies that do not sell shares to the public (for example C & J Clark, which makes Clark's and K Shoes), and there are many large partnerships (for example, the big accountancy firms), most large businesses in Britain are public limited companies or 'PLCs'.

When this book refers to 'company', this is usually what it is talking about.

The Principles of Company Law

The elements of the modern form of business company were laid down in law in the 1850s. They have since evolved into the following basic principles:

The Company. Companies are set up, or 'incorporated', by people wishing to associate for a particular business purpose. But once they are incorporated companies become more than simple associations of people; they become 'legal persons' on their own account. That is to say they become abstract legal entities, independent of their founder members. According to legal convention these entities can enter into contracts, employ people, own property, commit crimes, sue and be sued. As such, they have in some ways the same sort of legal status as a real person. While all companies operate within the same legal framework, they each have a distinct legal 'personality,' which is defined by the members by drawing up two legal documents: the 'memorandum of association' and the 'articles of association'. As legal entities, companies are in many respects independent of their directors, shareholders and employees, although for certain purposes the company can be identified with these groups of people.

The Directors. Depending on the circumstances, the law considers directors to be variously the controllers, agents, alter egos, and servants of the company. The board of directors is expected by the law to exert day-to-day company control. While the board has this duty, it can, and usually does, appoint officers (from among its members and elsewhere) to exert practical daily supervision; the most prominent of these is the chief executive. But, while these appointed officers manage the company, the articles of association confer overall control over the companies activities and policy on the board of directors as a whole. As a corollary of this power, the Companies Act gives the board formal responsibilities to its shareholders, its employees and the company as a whole.

The Shareholders. Shareholders are members of the company. In legal terms they are not fully its owners. The shareholders, meeting together annually, are expected to oversee the activities of directors, approve the appointment of directors and may dismiss them. They may also alter the articles of association, and, in some companies, may direct the board to follow specific policies. So, in theory at least, the shareholders as a body have ultimate long-term control of the company.

These are the three central participants in British company law. Their legal relationship embodies the basic principles of ownership, control and accountability in company law. It is noteworthy that groups of people such as the employees, the consumer and the public at large do not have a substantial place in company law.

The legal framework that has evolved over the last hundred and fifty years has been hugely successful at enabling business to operate profitably. A considerable proportion of the spectacular economic growth that has occurred in the West in the last hundred years can be put down to the invention of the incorporated limited company. However, while the invention of the corporation has been remarkably productive at an economic level, serious questions exist about the wide discrepancies between the legal theory and actual corporate practice, and more generally about role of companies in modern society. Chapter 3 will look at these questions and assess the various calls for legal and structural reform in British corporate governance. This section examines the legal framework as it stands now.

The Independent Legal Personality of the Company

On incorporation, the company becomes a body corporate, a legal person enjoying the historic attributes of corporate status. These include the power to sue and be sued in its own name, the right to hold and alienate its own property, and perpetual succession . . . As a general rule, a company is governed by directors who are chosen by the members. The directors are vested with the executive government of the company while the shareholders enjoy a residual power. But, although the shareholders are members of the company, having ultimate power of control, and although the directors manage it, the company is a legal entity separate and distinct form its members and directors.[11]

The incorporation of a company represents a mysterious legal transition. Before incorporation a firm is just a group of people carrying out their business, they make the profits and bear the risk of their business. After incorporation, the group of people remain but their business is legally carried out by another entity, a legal company, which makes the profits and faces the risks. On incorporation a new legal 'person' is born. The principle that the company is a legal person, independent of its shareholders, its directors and its employees, is the source from which most of the rest of company law flows.

The Saloman Case

The separate legal identity of companies was notionally established by legislation in the 1850s. The dramatic implications of this fact were not, however, properly appreciated until the end of the century in the celebrated case of Saloman *v.* Saloman & Co. Ltd. This case produced great outrage at the time. The story is as follows. Mr Saloman owned and ran a successful leather business. In 1892 he set up an incorporated, limited company, Saloman & Co. Ltd., to run the business. However, before the incorporated company could officially control the business, the law required a legal game to be played. Mr Saloman was not allowed to simply declare that his business would henceforward be run by his company. Instead the incorporated company had to go through the motions of buying Mr Saloman's business from him. The price Mr Saloman valued his business at was £39,000. The figure was fairly arbitrary and bore little relation to the actual market value of the leather business. As the company had only just been set up, it had no money of its own yet. So, under the instruction of Mr Saloman, its director, it issued 40,000 £1 shares. Mr Saloman himself bought 20,001 of the shares, his family bought another six; leaving the rest unsold. The company, run by Mr Saloman, now had £20,007 in capital which it could pay Mr Saloman for his business. However, because Mr Saloman had only bought half the shares, the company was still nearly £20,000 short of the purchase price. So the company made up part of the difference by giving Mr Saloman £10,000 in 'debentures'. A debenture is a kind of written guarantee that someone owes someone else some money. In this case the company undertook that it owed Mr Saloman £10,000, secured on the assets of the company. The business remained exactly the same as it had always been, except that previously it was run by Mr Saloman, now it was run by an incorporated company which Mr Saloman controlled.

However, quite soon afterwards the company failed, due to lengthy strikes during which it built up quite high debts. The company's creditors forced the company to close so they could get back at least some of the money they had lent to it. However, there were now two types of debt that the company owed: secured debt that it had issued guarantees for (Mr Saloman's £10,000 in debentures); and more casual, unsecured debt that it had not issued written guarantees for. The creditors all held the second kind of debt.

Once Mr Saloman produced his written guarantees he was legally entitled to demand that he be repaid in full by the company, before any of the other creditors (who did not hold guarantees) got a penny. This was somewhat audacious considering that the 'debt' that the company owed Mr Saloman was based on Saloman's dreamt-up price for his leather business, and had not required Mr Saloman to part with any money. This notwithstanding, Mr Saloman got his money before the unsecured creditors and, as there was not enough money to go around, these other creditors were left unpaid.

The creditors petitioned the Appeal Court, arguing that this was unfair, that the company was a sham, and that it was simply a front for Mr Saloman. They implied that Saloman and his company were effectively the same. They suggested that Saloman was engaged in a devious ploy to avoid paying his debts to his creditors. The Court of Appeal accepted the argument that the company was merely an alias for Mr Saloman, and ruled in favour of the other creditors. However the House of Lords overturned the appeal decision. The question was stark: either the company was a legal entity or it was not. As Saloman & Co. Ltd. had been incorporated in the correct manner under the law, it was a separate legal entity. Despite the fact that Mr Saloman was both the controlling shareholder, and the managing director of the company, he was not the company. The company was 'at law a different person altogether' from Mr Saloman, and this is the principle that has remained. Companies are considered by the law to be different 'people' from those people who own and control them. This ruling enabled Mr Saloman, and many businessmen since, to survive the collapse of their businesses at the expense of their creditors.

A similar and more bizarre case involved a Mr Lee, who set up his own flying company, of which he was the sole shareholder and managing director. He was also the chief pilot of the company. Under Mr Lee's direction, the company took out an insurance policy to cover its workers against injury. Mr Lee subsequently died in an air crash. His wife applied to the insurance company for compensation. But there arose some question about whether the insurance company should compensate Mrs Lee under its policy. The company argued that the policy only applied to 'servants' of the company, and as Mr Lee was managing director, and so master of the company, he could hardly be called a servant. However the final appeal court ruled that, as managing director of the company, Mr Lee could, on the company's behalf, give *himself* orders in his capacity as chief pilot. So he was a servant of the company, as well as its master, and in effect master and servant of himself. The reason why this logical nonsense seemed acceptable to the court was because the legal person of the company stood between Mr Lee, the managing director, and Mr Lee, the chief pilot. This case is a good example of the function of the invisible legal entity of the company, enshrined in English law. The case added strength to the Saloman judgement, that companies are autonomous legal beings.

In more recent times there has been some weakening of the legal personality principle, but in general the courts accept that the company is an independent legal entity and not an agent or an alias of the shareholders, or their appointees — the directors. There are exceptions, however, such as when a company is clearly being used as a front to hide criminal activity. Also, as we shall see below, the law is also sometimes ready to consider the company an agent of its shareholders if its dominant shareholder is another company.

The Effects of
Independent Legal Personality

There are many things which follow from the law's treatment of the company as an artificial person. They include:

1. *Limited Liability.* If a company is a separate legal entity, then it follows that it should be responsible for its own debts, in the same way that real people are responsible for their own debts. If the company is liable for its debts then the shareholders cannot be, or so the argument goes. But the law

does not go quite this far. Companies tend to be 'limited by shares' this means that shareholders are liable for their company's debts up to the value of their shares.

2. *Perpetual Succession.* Companies, unlike real people, are not mortal, and so can exist indefinitely. As shareholders and directors come and go, the company remains, unperturbed. Moreover, even if the business it represents fails, the company can still remain, in limbo, on the register of companies in Companies House; where it may be bought for a small charge by some new entrepreneurs, saving them the difficulty of going through the bureaucracy of creating a new company.

3. *Property Ownership.* Companies, as legal people, can own property, including shares in other companies, on their own account. In this case the company itself owns property, independently of its shareholders. Its ownership is absolute and the shareholders do not have any direct proprietary rights over the company's property.

4. Companies can sue in their own name and they can also be sued. If someone wants to sue an unincorporated body they must sue the individual members of that body, not the body itself. Company bodies may themselves be sued, making legal action more straightforward.

5. Other consequences of incorporation are that companies can enter into contracts, they can commit crimes and they are taxed on their own account.

All these consequences of incorporation follow as a matter legal convention. They are compatible with the assumption that the company should be treated as a person. But it is important to remember that a company is patently *not* a person. A company, after all, has no body, no mind, no personality and no presence to speak of. So how can it own things? How can it employ people? How can it sign contracts? How can it break the law?

The law has developed a complicated set of conventions to deal with these questions. This kind of convention-making is what legal institutions do all the time, to cope with the numerous abstractions they are forced to deal with. For example, when 'Britain' is at war, it would be hard to pin down precisely what is at war, but nevertheless international law has conventions that define what this means. Similarly the law has conventions that govern the concept of the company as a legal person.

Companies Without Bodies

When the company exercises its legal rights to own property, or to make contracts, it does not do so in person because quite obviously it has no 'person'. Instead it carries out its activities through its agents. These generally speaking are the company's directors and their appointees. But, in the everyday world, agents are appointed by the person for whom they are to act, in this case the company. This raises a problem: how can a ghostly legal entity like a company appoint agents? The legal convention adopted to get round this problem is to say that the shareholders in a general meeting are counted *as* the company for the purpose of appointing its agents. But shareholders cannot meet every time the company needs to appoint someone to act as its agent. So the law has also adopted the idea that the board of directors, appointed by the shareholders, can appoint agents on behalf of the company.

In some cases, however, the law goes further than assuming that the people who act on behalf of the company are its agents. As the following House of Lords ruling in 1915 suggests, the law sometimes assumes people acting for the company to actually be the company.

> My Lords, the corporation is an abstraction. It has no mind of its own any more than it has a body of its own; its active and directing will must consequently be sought in the person of somebody who for some purposes may be called an agent, but who is *really the directing mind and will* of the corporation, the very ego and centre of the personality of the corporation . . . [12]

So, for example, when a crime is committed, it is often important for the prosecution to prove that the accused was acting with criminal intent, rather than committing the crime by accident. If a company is accused of breaking the law, how can anyone prove that a notional legal entity has criminal intent? The legal convention adopted to overcome this problem is to assume that the mind of the company is, for practical purposes, the mental state of those people controlling its actions. Thus, if the people responsible for a management decision that resulted in a crime taking place can be shown to have had criminal intent, then the company is ascribed criminal intent. If the chief executive has criminal intentions, then by convention the company has criminal intentions too. One limitation on this principle is that only those people appointed by the directors as 'responsible officers'[13] count for these purposes. Another fact that is worth noting is that the identification between company officers and the company acts both ways. If a company is found to be criminally liable, then the officers concerned will be presumed liable too.

In summary, depending on the particular requirements, the law sometimes substitutes the will of the majority of shareholders for that of the company, at others it substitutes the will of the board, and at others it substitutes the will of individual company officers for that of the company. As Lord Justice Denning said,

> A company may in many ways be likened to a human body. It has a brain and a nerve centre which controls what it does. It also has hands which hold the tools and act in accordance with directions from the centre. Some of the people in the company are mere servants and agents who are nothing more than hands to do the work and cannot be said to represent the mind or will. Others are directors and managers and represent the directing mind or will of the company and control what it does. The state of mind of these managers is the state of mind of the company . . . [14]

This principle is sometimes known as the organic theory. It should be remembered that it does not apply to all cases. Sometimes the normal laws of agency apply: for example, when officers exceed the authority that the company has given them it is considered doubtful whether their actions can be considered to be those of the company. The law in this area is quite complex. The main point that can be taken from this section is that the law has a flexible, pragmatic attitude to the legal personality of the company. For some purposes the company is seen as entirely separate from its controllers and its owners, while for others it is seen as identical with them. The next sections will look at specific examples of this flexibility.

The Process of Incorporation

The process that gives birth to a company is called incorporation. People can trade very successfully either on their own or in partnership with others without forming a company. However, particularly for large businesses, there are many advantages that derive from incorporating as a company. Most companies are first incorporated as private companies and become public later, once they have grown in size. The actual process of incorporation involves the drafting of two documents: the memorandum of association and the articles of association; followed by their submission for approval by the Registrar of Companies, at Companies House.

The Memorandum and Articles of Association

Company law sets the limits of the legal personality of the company, within which it allows a wide degree of freedom about the more detailed constitution of individual companies. The individual constitution of each company is layed down by its founder members at the time of incorporation, in the form of the memorandum of association and the articles of association.

The memorandum states the name and status of the company and sets out its purpose and its powers. The memorandum is the document from which a company derives its most basic legal existence. The memorandum is also an important document because it sets the details of the company's name, powers and business purposes which must be stuck to. The statement of purpose or 'objects' must state, plainly and unambiguously, all the kinds of business activities that the company will be involved in. While the objects must be adhered to they may later be changed in certain legally defined ways by a special resolution at a shareholders' meeting.

The articles of association supplement the memorandum by setting out in much greater detail the internal administrative rules by which a company is to conduct its business. They are secondary to the memorandum and must follow it. The Companies Acts contain standard articles of association. Companies can adopt these unchanged or they may produce their own. Generally speaking, companies tend to broadly follow the articles suggested by 'Table A' of the Companies Act, 1985. Any divergences must follow minimum standards set out in the rest of company law. The articles can be changed, with certain restrictions, by special resolutions at a shareholders' meeting. These require a three-quarters majority of shareholders in order to be passed. The articles are, in practical terms, the most important document in the company. In the articles the members of the company lay down the scope of the directors' authority. The articles divide the powers the directors can exercise in the board room, from those reserved for the shareholders' meeting. It is advisable for shareholder activists to obtain copies of company articles, as they set out the general procedures to be followed at shareholders' meetings and define the scope of shareholder tools like resolutions. There are in many cases wide divergences between the standard procedures, outlined in this book, and those specified by the articles of some companies. The articles of association of individual companies can be obtained from Companies House for a small fee.[15]

The Directors

The directors have a very important role in the company. This role is far from straightforward. Because of the numerous conventions adopted by company law, the directors have a number of different kinds of relationship with the company. They are variously agents, controllers, trustees and *alter egos* of the company, and they may also be its servants and members. The importance of directors consists in the fact that, under the law, overall day-to-day corporate control is expected to be exercised by the board of directors, rather than by shareholders. Corresponding to this power, the law imposes various duties on the directors. These are: 'fiduciary' duties of loyalty and good faith, duties of care and skill, and statutory duties of disclosure. Fiduciary is a legal term that denotes a relationship of trust.

Loyalty and Good Faith

The directors' fiduciary duty is often referred to as a duty of loyalty and good faith. In law, people in a fiduciary position should behave honestly, fairly and should not abuse their position. In the case of companies, directors owe their fiduciary duty to 'the company as a whole'. This has been taken to include, variously, the legal entity of the company (although one might question how an abstract legal entity can be in a relationship of trust with anybody), the present and future shareholders of the company, the creditors, and the 'interests of the employees in general'.[16] The interests of these groups often conflict, and the law does not give clear guidance in dealing with such conflicts. There is too little space here to examine fully the complexities of the legal debate.

One area of contention is whether the directors owe any duties to other groups who have a stake in the company. These 'stakeholders' may include the consumers, the suppliers, the community in which the company operates, and the environment. A common response of directors to appeals on behalf of these stakeholders, is that the directors are not *allowed* to respond to stakeholder concerns. This, they argue, is because the directors have an over-riding duty to shareholders, to increase the value of shares. This is a bit too simple. The duty is to the company as a whole, of which the present shareholders only form a part. But in a sense the directors are right, the law is quite clear that directors' fiduciary responsibilities do not extend to the other stakeholder groups. Whether or not the law *should* take this position is open to debate.

In any case, as L.C.B. Gower says, 'as long as the company remains a going concern the members' interests will normally be served by having regard to the other [stakeholder] interests; rebellious staff, hostile trades unions, dissatisfied customers and an aggrieved public . . . are not conducive to the future prosperity of the company.'[17] So there is usually a good case to be made for directors paying out to charity and to protect the environment, on the grounds that it is good for long term profitability — therefore good for the company as a whole. Another similar argument as to why directors should appear to be behaving responsibly in areas of public concern is that it helps to avert any new, tougher legislation which would otherwise be imposed. While it may be prudent for the directors to act in the interests of other stake-holders, however, it is not their legal duty to do so.

There are several specific obligations directors have as a result of their fiduciary duties. Among these are the requirements that they must act in the best interests of the company; they must only use the powers which the company has conferred upon them, without exceeding them, even if they think it is in the best interests of the company to do so; and they must not put themselves in a position where there is potential conflict between the interests of the company and their own interests.

One possible exception to the general rule that directors must act solely in the best interests of the company is in the case of nominee directors. Nominee directors are appointed by special interest groups on the company like large shareholders, banks with large loans to the company, or even, potentially, shareholder activists. Such nominees are obviously nominated to look after the interests of the person who nominated them. However the law expects all directors to act in the best interests of the company, not a specific group. So the law will not allow directors to be puppets of any interest group. However, if this is taken too strongly, it makes it pointless to appoint nominee directors to look after particular interests. This question remains unresolved by the law.

Care and Skill

The duties of care and skill are rather less exacting than those of loyalty and good faith. Directors have to display the degree of skill that can reasonably be expected of them, taking into account their particular areas of experience and expertise. A director with no background in finance would not, therefore, be expected to understand and control the fine detail of the company's accounts. This obligation of directors is not full-time. Directors are not required to continuously monitor the activities of the company. They are only required to give their time at board meetings, and they are not even obliged to attend all of these. Directors may delegate all the duties that the articles of association do not require them to do themselves, to other 'officers' in the firm.

Duties of Disclosure

In addition to these general duties, directors are responsible for delivering the annual report and accounts to the registrar of companies and to the shareholders. If they do not, or are late, they can all be personally fined, disqualified, or even held criminally liable.

Roles of Directors

The directors' fiduciary responsibility makes them in a limited sense trustees of the company. However, the more important role directors serve is as agents of the company. It used to be the common legal opinion that the general meeting of shareholders in some senses *is* the company. At this meeting the shareholders acting *as* the company could therefore appoint directors as agents to act in their place. More recently, the

idea that the directors are agents of the shareholder meeting
has become less influential. It is now considered that the relationship depends entirely on the company's articles of association. The articles can severely limit the ability of
shareholders to tell the directors what to do. This weakens
the principle of agency, as it is difficult to consider someone
your agent if you cannot tell them what to do. Consequently,
rather than being agents of the shareholders' general meeting,
under some interpretations the law conceives the relationship
between the shareholders at the general meeting and the directors to be contractual.[18] For example, the shareholders
may feel that if they agree to let the managers manage, without shareholder interference, then the company will be better
off financially. If they so agree, this agreement may be contractually enshrined by adopting a form of articles which prevent shareholder interference in matters of general
management policy. Once bound by this contract, the shareholders can change the articles by a three-quarters majority
vote at a shareholders' meeting but, short of that, they are
prevented form interfering. Directors under these circumstances have every right to ignore shareholders' instructions
that relate to company policy issues. This has important implications for shareholder action, but it has larger consequences because it means that the articles of association can
give the directors a source of authority at one remove from
the shareholders. So, rather than the power being held by the
shareholders' meeting, with the directors merely agents, in
practice the directors form a second centre of power in the
company. And, as we shall see in subsequent chapters, the directors are in many ways the dominant centre of power.

Nevertheless, while the agency principle is weakened in this
way, the idea that the directors are agents of the company
still applies. And when it does so, the power of agency is considered to be held by the directors when meeting together as
a board, and not by directors as individuals. While individual
directors are not agents, they can be appointed as such by the
board. This appointment need not be explicit. If for example
a director is placed by the board in a position which requires
him or her to act as an agent, then the power of agency will
be assumed. When a director, or an officer appointed by a director, is acting within the powers given to them, they are
considered agents of the company and agreements they make
are binding on the company, and the company is liable for
them.

It is usual for the board to appoint a managing director or chief executive. This usually entails that the board transfers large areas of its powers partially or exclusively to the managing director. Between board meetings, the managing director is the effective ultimate authority in the company. The managing director in some companies is extremely powerful, to the extent that the companies are effectively controlled by just one person. While this arrangement allows greater flexibility than the 'management by committee' preferred by some companies, it is widely acknowledged to be a dangerous state of affairs, with great potential for abuse of power — as the late Robert Maxwell amply demonstrated.

Directors are not, in their role as directors, employees or servants of the company. But often individual directors are contracted to serve as officers of the firm. Some directors known as executive directors, are employed as members of staff by the company. As such these executive directors have contractual duties to the company in addition to their basic directoral responsibilities.

As mentioned previously, companies can be prosecuted for committing crimes. One of the general conditions for a successful criminal prosecution is evidence that there existed in the mind of the criminal a wilful intent to commit the crime. Legal entities like companies cannot have intentions; so the courts consider the thoughts of the directors or of the other company officers to be the intentions of the company. In such circumstances the directors are not considered servants or agents of the criminal company; they are actually considered to be its *alter ego*. Their criminal intentions become the criminal intentions of the company. Consequently, if on this basis the company is found to have commited a crime, then those directors responsible are also criminal; to the extent that if a company is found guilty the directors will also be assumed to be guilty, unless they can show that they had nothing to do with the crime.

It is common for a company's articles of association to require that a proportion of the directors must retire each year. It is also common for most of these retiring directors to offer themselves for re-election. The permanent retirement age for directors is 70, although exceptions can be made. The directors are elected by shareholders by a first-past-the-post system, like the House of Commons, not proportional representation. In other words 51% of shareholders can appoint the whole board with no representation for interests of the other 49%. Some countries, and many American states, do have some form of proportional representation, where minority shareholder groups are able to get some directors on the board.

It is worth making one point about the relationship between the directors and the shareholders. It sometimes happens at shareholder meetings that an irate shareholder stands up and orders a director to do something, on the basis that director is the shareholder's employee. This not the case. While directors are appointed by the shareholders, they are not employed by them. Directors, in the role as directors, are *not* the employees of the company, they are the company's controllers. Although, as mentioned above, 'executive' directors are employed by the company. But even this does not make them employees of the shareholders. As has been stated earlier the company is separate from its shareholders, although they do have some rights of ownership.

Other Officers

In addition to the directors, the law defines the company secretary and senior management as company officers. Company officers are considered, to varying degrees, similar to the directors in terms of their duties and liability. Company officers are servants of the company, but they can be its agents, *alter egos* and members. For some purposes the law also defines the accountant and auditor as officers of the company. Company officers are agents of the company and can be held liable for the activities of the company.

The Shareholders: Ownership versus Membership

Shareholders are not, in the eye of the law, part owners of the undertaking [the company]. The undertaking is something different from the totality of the shareholdings.[19]

This ruling by Lord Justice Evershed in 1948 is quite explicit. In the strictest legal terms, shareholders do not own companies, despite the common impression to the contrary. In fact, under the law, no one owns the legal entity of the company. So the term 'share' can be misleading, because the ownership of a share does not mean that the shareholder owns a part share of the company. Instead share ownership represents a share in the 'share capital' of a company and conveys on the owner entitlement to certain limited rights. The share capital is the store of capital which companies need to run and develop their business. The whole thrust of the idea of incorporation is that the corporate entity is a legal *person*, which cannot be a mere item of property.

The law also considers the shareholders' relationship with the company is a contractual one. The law thinks of a share as a 'chose in action'. The word 'chose' merely means 'thing', and the term applies to a loose collection of things such as copyrights, patents and trade marks. This distinguishing feature of this class of legal things is that they confer certain rights to their owner, but no rights to the possession of a physical object. A patent, for example, gives rights over an original design; a copyright gives rights over ideas, themes or plots. This implies that shares confer legal rights to their owners, but not rights of possession over a physical object. These rights are of a contractual form and they are between the shareholders and the legal entity of the company. The contract is between the shareholders as a group and the company, and is defined by the articles of association.

A further, rather simpler, alternative is to consider shareholders as 'members' of companies, rather than their owners. From this perspective, shareholders, on buying shares, become members of an association. This gives them rights defined by the articles of association, to participate in the deliberations of the 'company' of people associating to pursue their mutual business interests. In this respect, shareholders behave more like the members of large organisations, like unions or political parties, than as the owners of property. This is emphasised by the fact that:

1. Shareholders can only exercise the majority of their powers when they meet together, usually at the annual general meeting (AGM). They do not have many rights that can be effectively exercised on an individual level outside the framework of the shareholder meetings. Almost all the actions that the law allows shareholders to take must be *collectively* taken at company meetings.

2. Shareholder rights are not general in their scope, like the general rights people have when they own something. If you own a piece of furniture, say, as long as you do not hurt anyone or commit public indecency, you can do pretty much what you like to it and the law will not intervene. Individual

shareholders cannot do what they like with companies. The scope of their action is tightly circumscribed by the law and limited contractually by the company's articles of association.

As mentioned in the previous chapter, the word 'company' comes from the same Latin root as 'companion', and originally meant a group of people associating together in order to pursue a particular shared purpose. The interpretation of shareholders as members of a company, associating together to pursue a particular purpose, fits this better than that of shareholders as owners.

Despite these kinds of argument and the judicial ruling that heads this section, there is a widespread opinion that shareholders do own companies. This opinion is held by many influential members of the British financial community. For example, the recent draft report of the Cadbury Committee on The Financial Aspects of Corporate Governance said that 'the shareholders *as owners* of the company elect the directors to run the business on their behalf and hold them accountable for its progress.'[20] This puts the financial community at odds with the lawyers; this book can, however, devote no more space to the legal and philosophical issues raised by this difference of opinion.

Classes of Shares

While the majority of company shares are ordinary voting shares, different classes of shares can be issued if the power to do so has been written into the articles of association. Different classes of shares carry different rights and different rewards. Among the various kinds are:

1. *Preference shares*, which give holders preferential treatment over dividends, but often deny them voting rights.

2. *Ordinary shares* without voting rights, which carry the usual dividend rights but deny shareholders any right to vote.

3. *Founders/deferred shares*, often with weighted voting rights; these for example allow the founder to keep voting control over the company, while holding less than 50% of the capital.

4. *Redeemable shares*, which are shares that the company can buy back. They are commonly issued within the framework of employee share options schemes, so that when the employee leaves the company they can be repurchased

and allocated to a new employee. The specific rights of redeemable shares vary.

It is worth noting that redeemable shares are an exception to rule that companies are not generally allowed to buy their own shares. If companies could buy their own shares, they would be able to artificially manage their own share prices; and they could also buy up all their own shares, leaving them with total control of *themselves*. Redeemable shares, however, can be bought by companies, but carry certain restrictions which are supposed to prevent these kinds of abuse.

The Rights of Shareholders

Most shareholders in publicly listed companies have ordinary voting shares. The legal minimum rights of these shareholders are:

1. To attend shareholders' meetings.

2. To bring resolutions before the meetings.

3. To vote on the appointment of directors.

4. To vote on the appointment of auditors.

5. To approve the directors' report and accounts.

6. To vote on any other resolutions brought before the meeting.

7. To ask questions of the board of directors.

The bulk of these shareholder rights are exercised collectively at shareholders' meetings. This is reflected by the fact that the law considers the shareholders' meeting to be a company's ultimate source of control. While the board of directors is relied upon to carry on the company's day-to-day business, it is with the shareholders' meeting that ultimate authority is supposed to rest. It is worth emphasising that the law does not consider ultimate power to rest with individual shareholders as such, but only with the collective body of shareholders at a properly convened shareholders' meeting. The collective body of shareholders attending general meetings in person is usually only a small proportion of the total body of shareholders. Yet the decisions taken by the shareholders attending the meeting, together with the appointed representatives of shareholders not present, are binding on all the shareholders.

The directors must convene a shareholders' meeting at least once each calender year, and no later than fifteen

months after the previous meeting. This meeting is the standard 'annual general meeting', but if it is necessary, other 'extraordinary meetings' can be called. Directors can convene
extraordinary meetings at will, shareholders may only do so
if they control 10% of the voting shares.

The shareholders, when meeting together, in theory have
very extensive rights to control the policy of the company at
the general meeting. The primary restriction on these rights
is that shareholders are barred from taking decisions which
the articles of association reserve specifically to the directors.
In some companies the articles reserve a considerable amount
of power for the directors; to the extent that shareholders are
not allowed to interfere at all in general business policy matters. As mentioned earlier, this means that even if shareholders pass a resolution on a general policy issue, the directors
are entitled to ignore it. This kind of constraint can only occur if specified by the articles of association. The articles are
approved and can be altered by the shareholders. So if the articles proscribe shareholder interference, it is because previously shareholders have adopted a form of articles which
limits their own powers.

Voluntary arrangements of this kind are quite common and
arise because, at some stage in the past, the shareholders
have been convinced that they will benefit if they constrain
their ability to interfere with management matters. So there
are many British companies in which the shareholders have
agreed to tie their hands behind their back. As Peter Morgan,
director general of the Institute of Directors has argued: 'The
responsibility for running the company is that of boards of directors' and that while shareholders have their role 'questions
of governance are determined in the board room'.[21] The Cadbury report takes a more shareholder-oriented line, and as we
shall see in Chapter 3, there is currently a tug-of-war in progress over the relative powers of directors and shareholders
in the company.

A further right of shareholders, based on the fact that they,
together with the company's creditors, are supplying the company's capital, is that shareholders are entitled to a share of
any assets remaining when the company is wound up.

During a takeover battle, shareholders have the right to decide to collectively sell their shares to the predatory company, or to come to some other arrangement. If a takeover
bid is successful and the shareholders sell their shares to the
predatory company, it is common to assume that the shareholders are 'selling' the company, implying that they own it.

in fact in legal terms they are selling their shares rather than the company itself; for a sum of money they are transferring their legal rights of *control* in the company to the takeover company.

More details of these shareholder rights, and the regulations covering their use are covered in Chapter 8 on Formal Action at AGMs.

The Role of the Shareholders

A large part of company law exists in order to prevent shareholders' interests from being abused by company directors. This most significant legal protection for shareholders is the requirement that the directors produce a detailed annual report of their activities, together with audited accounts. The need to protect shareholders is also the basis for the requirement for the directors to call the shareholder's general meeting annually, and for the directors to offer themselves regularly to the shareholders for re-election.

The point of these protective requirements is to give the shareholders the information they require to assess the state of their company's affairs, to ensure that the directors are behaving satisfactorily and, if not, to act upon their dissatisfactions. By implication the shareholders are expected to play an active part in the regulation of their companies, using their legal rights to make sure that their interests are indeed protected. Judging from the public activities of shareholders at AGMs, there is little evidence that this happens to any great degree. Few tough questions are asked of directors at annual general meetings; almost all directors are re-elected, regardless of their performance; and most shareholders do not pay enough detailed attention to the report and accounts to make any proper judgement about the state of their company — although even a close reading tends to give only a partial understanding of the company's affairs. Consequently, when big companies collapse, or experience considerable financial difficulty, the common shareholder reaction is to complain loudly 'the regulators' have failed to do their job. Shareholders conveniently forget that, in the eyes of the law, they are the primary regulators of companies.

One of the central principles of company law is that companies should be self-regulating to some degree. That is to say that the shareholders, in looking after their own interests, should be leading the regulation of companies. The other regulators should be supplementing the shareholders' regulatory role. To this end, the law envisages that shareholders will be able and inclined to occupy an overseeing role over the board of directors; periodically approving the directors' actions, and assuring themselves that the directors are going about their company's business in a satisfactory way. This legal theory is not mirrored in practice. The next chapter will explore some of the problems, and some of the suggestions for reform.

Chapter 3
Corporate Governance Reform

Self-Regulation

Companies are managed by their directors, who are appointed by the shareholders. The shareholders entrust the directors with running the company's business on their behalf. This trust is backed up by the directors' legal responsibility to act in the best interests of the company as a whole, which is generally, but not exclusively, taken to mean the interests of shareholders as a group. From this legal principle comes the doctrine that the directors' prime responsibility is to increase 'shareholder value', by paying good dividends and enhancing the value of shares. In recent years there have been numerous calls for the directors also to have responsibilities to the employees, and the 1985 Companies Act answered these claims with an unspecific requirement that the directors look after the interests of the employees in general.[22]

If the directors follow their duties of loyalty and good faith, and care and skill, they should serve the interests of the company. However, in order to ensure this occurs, the directors' responsibility to shareholders is enforced by a system of accountability, in the form of the annual accounting process and the AGM. The shareholders are expected to use the annual report and accounts, and the forum provided by the AGM, to ensure that the directors are indeed working in the best interests of the company. This is the basic self-regulating model of the company that is central to the contemporary understanding of corporate governance. The assumption underlying it is that the shareholders, simply in order to protect their own interests, will want to scrutinise the activities of their directors, to make sure they are doing a good job.

The self-governance system has come under periodic criticism since it was initiated in the 1850s. The current pitch of concern reflects the wave of dramatic and unexpected company failures and frauds that have hit the City in recent years, notably the collapse of the Maxwell Corporation, Polly Peck and BCCI. In each of these collapses, company directors are implicated in malpractice. In each case, individual shareholders, employees, customers, pensioners or creditors have suffered loss as a result. There has also been considerable public concern about the rapidly rising salary levels of directors. In the last few years many directors have seen their salaries increase far in excess of the rate of inflation, despite falling company profits and despite successful attempts to hold down shop-floor pay rises to little more than the rate of inflation.

Governance Reform

Self-regulation is not the only form of supervision which companies face. There are a large number of legislative constraints within which companies and company directors must operate. In addition, companies are policed by a range of statutory and voluntary bodies, including the Department of Trade and Industry, the Serious Fraud Office, the Securities and Investments Board, the Stock Exchange, and the Bank of England. While the recent City scandals suggest the failure of these regulatory bodies to supervise companies adequately, underlying this failure is the absence of effective self-regulation within companies.

The system of self-regulation depends on the accountability of directors to shareholders. Accountability depends on extensive and reliable information being available to the shareholders, so that they can judge the performance of the directors and the company; together with the shareholders' willingness to use the information. Under the law this information is to be provided in the directors' report and accounts, to be published and laid before the shareholders at a general meeting, prior to which the accounts must be verified by the auditors. The directors' report and accounts are supposed to provide a true and fair view of the state of the company, but there have been considerable doubts raised about whether the current reporting arrangements guarantee this. In 1991 a review committee was set up under the chairmanship of Sir Adrian Cadbury, in response to the 'low level of confidence both in financial reporting and in the ability of auditors to provide the safeguards which the users of company reports sought and expected'.[23]

Two areas of common concern are:

1. The content and presentation of the accounts is not sufficiently clear, balanced or comprehensive to provide the information that shareholders need to judge the company's performance accurately.

2. The shareholders are unable or unwilling to use the available information and the opportunities they have to hold the directors accountable.

The first type of concern involves the various accounting standards, the legislation covering reporting, and the role of the auditors. As the draft report of the Cadbury committee says, with characteristic understatement:

Accounting standards and practice sometimes allow boards too much scope for presenting facts and the figures derived from them in a variety of ways. (Para. 5.3).

Often directors use this flexibility to present their activities as positively as possible, rather than presenting them as truthfully or as fairly as possible. The pursuit of the best possible 'treatment' of the accounts has led to reports and accounts which, although quite legal, are extremely misleading.

One might expect the auditors to be in a position to ensure that this does not happen; but there are a number of factors that prevent the auditors from doing their jobs properly. To begin with, the fact that such misleading accounts are still within the letter of the law makes it hard for auditors to condemn them. But there are other possible reasons why auditors are reluctant to act. Auditors are hired not by the shareholders but by the directors, although their appointment must be approved by the shareholders. Consequently they have a business relationship with the directors, and as the Cadbury report puts it, 'audit firms, like any other business, will wish to have a constructive relationship with their clients'.[24] The report goes so far as to acknowledge that the auditors are competing to meet the needs of their clients, the directors, at the expense of meeting the needs of the shareholders. This is because the auditors need to ingratiate themselves with the directors in order to get and retain business, rather than trying to satisfy the shareholders' needs. Auditors who regularly reject the directors' attempts to present their accounts a shade too positively, are not likely to find it easy to maintain their audit contracts. Directors will opt for softer, more easy-going auditors. So the incentive for auditors is to give the directors what they want and push the shareholders' needs to the back of their minds.

A further weakness is that currently companies tend to appoint the same auditor year after year, so close business relationships develop. The potential exists for these relationships between the auditors and their clients to become rather too amicable and 'constructive'. This problem is compounded by the fact that the major auditing companies are part of diversified accountancy, tax and management consultancy companies. The companies to which they are trying to sell auditing services are the same companies they are trying to sell these other services to as well. If auditors are too strict with their audit, their client companies might find that they no longer requires the auditors' lucrative management or tax consultancy services. It is also somewhat invidious for auditors in one company to audit the work of, say, tax consultants who are working for the same company.

The audit process is only part of the problem. Even if the accounts are properly audited and give a balanced view of the company's position, they are still beyond the capabilities of most shareholders to understand adequately. The complicated financial structures of modern, international companies are exceptionally hard to grasp fully. This is not helped by the proliferation of arcane accounting principles, legal jargon and wilful mystification. It is no surprise that research has shown that, instead of detailed examination of the company's financial data, shareholders tend to rely on the chairman's introductory statement at the shareholders meeting and in the annual report for their assessment of the company's performance. Yet the chairman's statement is not regulated or audited, so the chairman has even greater freedom to present his board's performance in the 'best positive light'.

The reforms which have been suggested to remedy some of these problems are:

● An audit of the chairman's statement, and legal requirements for the subjects that he must include.

● The prohibition of auditing companies selling other non-audit services to client companies.

● The requirement for companies to change their auditors every few years.

● Reformulation of accountancy standards to more strictly limit the scope for misleading accounting.

A further recommendation that will be referred to in more detail later, is the suggestion by the Cadbury committee that the board of directors set up auditing committees made up of independent, non-executive directors with powers to engage independent professional advice, to check that they accounts are true and fair. Of these possible reforms only the last two are expected to take place in the near future.

Failure of Shareholders

Companies have a democratic structure but the electorate does not vote. For example, the pension funds, as a group, are the largest investors on both sides of the Atlantic, but in the UK only 20% of them bother to vote at annual general meetings as a matter of course; the rest vote occasionally or not at all. The basic assumption behind the principle of account-ability, under-pinning self-regulation, is that shareholders should vote in order to protect their long-term interests. Yet most shareholders do not bother to do so and, even when they do, they rarely examine the issues closely. Consequently the overwhelming majority of shareholders do not participate actively in holding directors accountable. Annual reports go unread and most AGMs are anodyne occasions, with little scrutiny or interrogation of the directors.

The failure of shareholders is partly due do to the assumption that shares are financial investments that should bring rewards and not obligations — not unlike bank deposits. This results in a vicious circle: few investors perceive it to be their place to hold the directors to account, so few investors publicly challenge the directors, so, with so few examples of shareholders confronting directors to go on, few investors believe challenging directors is their role.

One of the things that perpetuates the circle is that the legal structure promoting the accountability of directors to shareholders is unreasonably restrictive. Anne Simpson, the joint managing director of PIRC, has said, that in order to take an active part in holding the directors accountable 'You need to be something of a zealot to battle your way through the red tape'. Alastair Blair, an institutional investment fund manager, who has attempted to fight through this red tape in the past has said,

> Many people have argued that institutions should act more quickly. However, the balance of power between managements and their shareholders is heavily skewed

in the former's favour, making quick action in most cases difficult, if not impossible.[25]

If a shareholder wants to take action using the tools the law provides, by calling shareholder meetings and proposing resolutions, that shareholder needs the support of several of the larger investors in the company. Gaining this support is difficult. And even if the support of, say, 15% of shareholders is achieved, the task has only just begun.

> There is . . . going to be a serious fight. You are not just challenging management decisions, but the very livelihoods of the managers . . . They have money on their side: the board will activate the whole corporate finance panoply — auditors, lawyers, merchant bankers, stockbrokers, public relations consultants. Each will depict a good management doing its best. Their presentations will be authoritative because they are based on hard information from inside the company . . . Meanwhile you are having to make your case without a battery of advisers. The company may be able to spend hundreds of thousands of pounds on professional fees, but your budget is likely to be close to zero.[26]

These are just some of the problems that shareholders face. There are a number of more technical legal difficulties which prevent shareholders from acting. If shareholders wish to bring a resolution to the shareholders' meeting, they must either have support of 5% of the voting shares or a total of 100 shareholders. In addition, they must submit the resolution at least six weeks in advance of the meeting, together with a 'requisition' that it be circulated to all the shareholders. The AGM date and agenda is decided by the directors. The directors are not required to announce the date of the AGM until 21 days before it takes place, which makes it impossible to work out the submission deadline for resolutions, because this is relative to the meeting date. Furthermore, the shareholders proposing the resolution are expected to pay for its circulation, which in certain circumstances can be very costly. These constraints, and other proceedures for the AGM, will be covered in more detail in Part Two of this book. In the light of these and other problems, it is perhaps unsurprising that shareholders in Britain have a reputation for being apathetic.

A clear example of shareholder apathy concerns the appointment of directors. Legally, the most significant aspect of the shareholder/director relationship is that the directors are

appointees of the shareholders. The shareholders are supposed to select and appoint individual directors, and dismiss
them if they do not perform adequately. In reality directors
tend to be invited onto the board by the chairman, with the
shareholders merely rubber-stamping the chairman's decision. Usually the chairman does not even think it worth both-
ering to make a case for his selection of a new director. This
has led to the situation where comings and goings of directors
to the board are not even noticed by the majority of shareholders. Furthermore, many shareholders, even large institutional ones, are no longer even aware of their role in the
appointment process. In a recent conversation, the director
of an institutional fund, responsible for investments of £400m,
expressed surprise at the present author's assertion that it is
the shareholders' duty to appoint the directors. He had the
conviction that it was the chairman's duty to appoint the directors, and that the shareholders had nothing to do with it.
The appointment of the directors is only one aspect in the
governance process, the lack of shareholder awareness ex-
tends to all other areas as well.

The Cadbury report acknowledges that the directors and
shareholders 'both have to play their part in making . . . accountability effective' and that shareholders should do this
'through their willingness to exercise their responsibilities as
owners'.[27] After all, the 'Shareholders have delegated many of
their responsibilities as owners to the directors who act as
their stewards. It is for the shareholders to call the directors
to book if they appear to be failing in their stewardship and
they should use this power.'[28] By implication, if the shareholders are unwilling or unable to exercise their responsibilities[29]
then there is a serious gap in the accountability process. The
draft Cadbury report offers a weak response to this problem.
It says that AGMs are a good opportunity for shareholders to
have

> direct public access to their boards. If too many annual
> general meetings are at present an opportunity missed,
> this is either because shareholders do not make the most
> of them or because boards do not encourage them to
> do so.[30]

But, other than the suggestion that both sides in the governance system should try harder, the Cadbury report has little
of substance to add. The suggestion that perhaps shareholder
committees should be set up to maintain regular contact with
the board, was rejected by the report because there are too

many conflicting interests among shareholders, which no committee could properly represent. So the report concluded that 'shareholders were in a better position to exercise their influence directly rather than through committees.'[31] Which seems to fly in the face of the fact that most shareholders seem unable to exercise much effective influence directly in any case.

Non-executive Directors and Accountability

Perhaps one reason why the Cadbury report is happy to be quiet on the issue of shareholder involvement, is that the report's emphasis is on accountability and supervision *within* the board of directors, rather than *of* the board of directors by shareholders. As a result, the report is full of recommendations for changing the way the board operates so that it is better at regulating itself. At the centre of the Cadbury vision for the future of corporate governance are the non-executive directors. The Cadbury principle is that executives are there to control the business and the non-executives are there to 'monitor the performance of the board'.

In many companies this does not tend to work. For a start, in some companies there are no non-executive directors on the board; but even when there are, they tend to be in a minority. In most companies there tends to be a rather 'cosy' relationship between the executives and the non-executives, this is because the non-executives are effectively appointed by the executive directors, they often receive substantial amounts of money from the company, and they often have business relationships with it. It is intriguing, for example, how many top companies have cross-directorships with each other. A cross-directorship is when an executive director in one company is a non-executive in another, and vice-versa. Even if explicit cross-directorships are not involved,

> non-executive directors are drawn almost exclusively from the boards of other listed companies. This can lead to a degree of peer group loyalty on issues such as executive pay, resulting in a 'you scratch my back and I'll scratch yours' syndrome.[32]

A further reason why the non-executives often fail to be effective is that the non-executives are often not in a position to judge what the executives are doing. The executive directors tend to control the non-executives' access to information about the company, and the non-executives often lack both the experience in the particular business areas in which the company operates, and the resources to properly investigate the executives' activities.

The Cadbury report recognises some of these problems and seeks to remedy them with some recommendations and a code of best practice. The report recommends that the non-executives bring 'independence of judgement' so they should be 'free of any business or financial connection with their company apart from their fees or their shareholding.'[33] And that 'the calibre and number of non-executive directors on a board should be such that their views carry significant weight in the boards decisions'.[34]

But the report does not go into details like how heavy is a significant weight? How high is sufficient calibre? How many is a sufficient number? And who should decide these things? The implication is that it is up to the board itself to decide. This does not seem a good way to guarantee the desired result. As mentioned above, there are some more specific recommendations about the setting up of an audit committee, composed of non-executive directors who have responsibility for checking that the report and accounts prepared by the executives provide a true and fair description. These audit committees, the report recommends, should have independent access to the auditors, and the right to hire independent financial advice at the company's expense. This is a good idea, provided the non-executives are genuinely independent and prepared to rock the boat on a regular basis. However, for reasons that have been pointed out above, non-executive directors are often not as independently minded as they need to be.

At the time of writing, the Cadbury report is only in its draft stage, it is likely to be revised somewhat. Any revisions that do take place are likely to be directed at weakening it rather than making it tougher. Once the final code is established, it may have some modestly threatening teeth: the code could be made a requirement for a market listing on the London Stock Exchange. A listing is indispensable for large companies, so the threat of withdrawing a listing is significant. Understandably, the question has been raised as to whether the Stock Exchange really would withdraw a listing from a company, since it would be catastrophic for its shareholders, who would thus have great difficulty selling their shares. Ultimately the report recognises 'that if companies do not back our recommendations, it is probable that legislation and external regulation will be sought to deal with some of the underlying problems which the report identifies."[35]

The committee which drafted the Cadbury report only had one shareholder representative, so it is perhaps unsurprising that the shareholder perspective is not fully expanded. It has been suggested that an essential supplement to the Cadbury code of practice would be structural and legal changes to allow shareholders greater opportunity to carry out their share in the corporate governance process.

The Charter for Shareholder Democracy

PIRC, which advises some of the most active institutional shareholders in the UK, has outlined a number of proposals for reform. The majority of these appeared first in 1991 in PIRC's Charter for Shareholder Democracy. Additions and revisions have subsequently been made, particularly in PIRC's submission to the Cadbury committee. The following lists the main ideas for reform.

● It should be considered a fiduciary duty for pension fund shareholders to independently exercise their voting rights in companies.

● Any shareholder holding 100 shares for at least one year should have the right to submit a resolution for consideration at the AGM. If the subsequent vote receives less than 3%, the resolution cannot be resubmitted for two years.

● The legitimate costs of properly formulated resolutions should be born by the company.

● Resolutions should be scrutinised by an independent body, to judge whether they are properly formulated.

● Companies should set AGM dates one year in advance.

● Annual reports should be sent to shareholders eight weeks in advance of the AGM, and should contain a reminder of the date of the meeting and an invitation to submit resolutions. Shareholders should then have another four weeks to submit resolutions to companies.

● The notice of the meeting, including notice of all properly submitted resolutions, should be circulated to shareholders four weeks before the meeting.

- Directors should expand on the issues that are put to the vote at the AGM for shareholder approval — to include those items which have significant impact on the company's progress or are significant externally (e.g. environmental liabilities and political donations).

- Companies should supply sufficient information to allow informed decision on votes — for example prospective directors should have to provide a biography and statement of their proposed role on the board.

- The quorum for AGMs should be raised, and should be based on a minimum proportion of shares rather than a minimum number of shareholders present. This should encourage large shareholders to attend.

- AGMs should not be brought to a close until all shareholders questions have been dealt with.

- After the AGM companies should be required to send a copy of the minutes of the meeting to shareholders.

These proposals serve to reduce greatly the structural impediments to shareholders taking action, and to enable the possibility of more lively and effective annual general meetings. Whether the charter will lead to 'shareholder democracy' rather than marginally increased shareholder power is another matter. The charter places the shareholders in a much more central position than the Cadbury committee does, but the accountability of directors still depends on the willingness of shareholders to be active in holding the directors to account. There have been questions of a more fundamental nature about whether shareholders can be expected to do this in modern companies, or even whether this is the right way to regulate companies.

Is Radical Reform Required?

One of the themes shared by those calling for more radical reform is that the control and accountability of companies should be more comprehensive and spread more widely than it is at the moment. At present the main formal vehicle for the accountability of directors is the company's annual general meeting. This meeting is, for the vast majority of companies, over in less than a couple of hours. It is absurd to expect shareholders, in the space of a few hours, to examine the directors in any detail about a company's diverse operations spread around the world, let alone to debate the many relevant issues involved. To do so would require annual general meetings to last several days, not several hours. Yet few shareholders can afford to spend days holding the directors of their companies accountable. This raises real questions about the appropriateness of regulation by shareholders.

There are other deeper questions about the propriety of regulation by the shareholders. Currently, the control and accountability of companies rest largely with shareholders and their appointees, the directors. While shareholders certainly have a stake in the company, they are not the only people who do so. The activities of Britain's large publicly quoted companies affect the welfare of everybody in Britain, and many groups of people have a special interest in the fortunes of each company. These groups include employees, consumers, suppliers, creditors, and the communities in which companies operate. Of these, the group whose claim to be represented on the board has had the most support is the employees.

Employees have some protection in the form of employment, equal opportunities, health and safety, and contract legislation, and an unspecified requirement in the Companies Act for the directors to look after their general interests. But employees do not have any formal involvement in the way companies are controlled: they do not appoint directors, and they may not decide company policy by putting resolutions to the annual general meeting. These rights are all reserved more or less exclusively to the shareholders.

One way that employees may gain a role in company control is by buying shares in the company. This has been encouraged by the proliferation of employee share-option schemes which allow employees to become shareholders. In some companies this approach has been taken further. In 1982, the employees of NFC, which operates the former British Road Services and the Pickfords removals and travel agency, bought the company from the government. Now, as the 1991 NFC Annual Review says,

> The essence of NFC's culture, employee ownership, reflects our belief that the people who work in the business should have the opportunity to own a stake in it, to share in the wealth created, and to take part in the strategic decision making process which determines its future.

In 1989 NFC was floated on the stock market, reducing the proportion of shares controlled by employees from 80% to less than 50%, but the employees still remain a very powerful lobby in the company. In the USA, employee share option schemes have made employees very powerful shareholder groups in a large number of companies. Recently, particularly with the large number of privatisations of public utilities, employees have been becoming a powerful lobby in British industry. In 1992 the GMB (General Municipal and Boilermakers union) coordinated an employee-shareholders campaign on some of the newly-privatised water companies. Its members nominated GMB representatives to the boards of directors of Thames Water PLC, North West Water PLC, and Anglian Water PLC. If elected, the proposed employee directors promised to raise a number of issues on the board, including cutting senior executives' pay, and providing regular reports to customers on environmental improvements and water quality. The nominations secured a third of the vote at Thames and North West, less at Anglia. The action by water company employees was facilitated by the fact that the water companies have a fairly common clause in their articles, one which allows a single shareholder to nominate a director.

While in Britain and the USA employees are gaining influence over company control by becoming shareholders, continental Europeans have, for several decades, opted for direct employee representation. A model for this approach is provided by Germany. Since 1861, German companies have been required to adopt a two-tier board structure. The top tier is a supervisory board, which controls the basic company policy, and the bottom tier is a management board which controls management matters and has day-to-day control (much like the British unitary board). The supervisory board is responsible for appointing the management board. In 1951 in the then West Germany, the supervisory boards of companies in the coal and steel industries were required by law to have half their number elected by employees. For other large companies the requirement was for one third to be employee representatives. This was increased to 50% for all companies in 1976. Today the highest authority in large German companies is elected, half by the shareholders and half by the employees. This structure is repeated in other European countries, and there are employee directors on the boards of many European companies. The European reasoning partly concerns the justice of allowing employees control over their lives, but partly the feeling that, if employees participate in the policy making of companies, there will be more of a sense of common purpose in the enterprise.

In 1977 the Labour government set up a royal commission to look into the question of employee involvement in companies, resulting in what became the Bullock Report on industrial democracy.[36] The majority verdict of this report was that British companies should move to a system of two-tier boards with an equal share of employee and shareholder directors. The report also recommended that the directors have a responsibility enshrined in Company Law to serve the interests of employees as well as the directors. In the event, by 1979 the Labour Party were out of government, and the Conservatives did not favour the suggested reforms. Nevertheless, the 1985 Company's Act did contain a clause giving the directors unspecified responsibilities to look after the interests of employees.

The reasons why Britain has not adopted the German system are complex, but perhaps the main argument has been that employee directors and two-tier boards would harm the efficiency of British companies. Superficially, at least, German companies and the German economy do not seem to have suffered overmuch as a result of this system. The response to this objection is usually a vague reference to the British having a different industrial culture to Germany, which somehow makes employee involvement at the board level inappropriate for us. It is difficult to see this as a decisive argument, now that the trade unions have largely dropped their anti-free-market agenda. It is ironic that the German system of 'co-determination' was instituted on the recommendation of the British occupation authorities in the British zone of post-war Germany, with the goal of reducing the chances that German industry should never again be in a position to support an extremist political party.[37]

The German system is the basis for the draft EC Fifth Directive on the harmonisation of company law. This directive, if implemented, would require EC companies with over 500 employees to have two-tier boards. The directive has since been watered down, and it is unlikely that Britain would be forced to adopt two-tier boards as a result. In certain limited respects British unitary boards already operate with a pseudo-two-tier structure (executive management directors and supervisory non-executive directors). If the Cadbury report is implemented, this feature will be amplified. So why not go all the way and adopt a two-tier approach, or alternatively allow employees to elect their representatives on to a unitary board, supplementing existing non-executive directors?

Another form of stakeholder representation-through-shareholding occurs through the pension funds.

> Pension funds and insurance companies control two thirds of the share capital of UK companies which places them in a position of responsibility for addressing corporate governance questions. They by turn are guardians of the collective savings of a wide selection of the community.[38]

Through their pensions and insurance premiums, many stakeholders have the possibility of exerting some influence on companies. Pension funds in particular offer opportunities for taking action on companies, but these are rarely exploited. Pension fund trustees are legally obliged to further the long term interests of the pension fund beneficiaries. In the past this has narrowly been interpreted to cover only the *financial* interest of beneficiaries. But this position is shifting. As PIRC argues, the shareholder voting rights which the trustees hold are an asset which should be managed with the same care and attention as the other pension fund assets.[39]

Currently much of the debate about company law reform is taking place in the space provided by the Cadbury committee's deliberations. The brief of this committee is fairly narrowly defined to include only the financial aspects of corporate governance. This serves to limit the scope of the governance debate. A more wide-ranging public discussion of the effectiveness of the whole self-regulation process would be extremely desirable, but this is unlikely to happen in the near future. It is likely that, once the final Cadbury report is published, many companies will take up many of the committee's recommendations, dampening the calls for more thoroughgoing legislative reform. However, as the committee acknowledges, this is unlikely to prevent the inevitability of substantial legal reform in the future.

Part Two
Shareholder Action

Chapter 4
Introduction to Shareholder Action

In Britain shareholder action has been carried out by a number of different kinds of actor, including:

1. Individuals.

2. Small national or local groups like PARTiZANS, Surfers Against Sewage, and End Loans to South Africa, with perhaps only one staff member and very limited resources.

3. Large, established, national pressure groups, with full-time staff and considerable resources and experience (e.g. Greenpeace and Friends of the Earth).

4. Institutional investors. (e.g. the South Yorkshire Pension Fund and the Church Commissioners).

5. Coalitions of institutional investors, pressure groups, and concerned individuals (e.g. the coalitions that campaigned on Shell and Barclays over South Africa, and more recently on Fisons over the digging of peat).

Small Scale Action

At the very minimum, if shareholders do not intend to attend their company's AGM, they can take action by simply returning the proxy appointment form that the company sends them, and indicating how they wish their vote to be used at the meeting. Currently in Britain a relatively small percentage of shareholders bother to return their proxy form. Shareholders who do so are at least fulfilling their most basic responsibility to participate in the corporate governance process.

If shareholders are unhappy with the board's performance in any way, they can register displeasure by indicating on the form that they oppose resolutions for the reappointment of directors, or for the adoption of the annual report. For a small shareholder, the message that this action sends is weak, but it is nevertheless a message that, if added to by other small shareholders, could become significant. More impact is generated by shareholders who return their proxy form accompanied by a letter explaining their decision to vote against the board.

Individual shareholders can take further action by writing occasional letters to the companies in which they own shares. These letters can simply express concerns, or ask for information about specific issues or company policies. This kind of action, while achieving a certain level of response, takes very little preparation. Companies do not get very many letters from their shareholders; consequently when they do so they tend to treat them seriously. An assumption made is that the number of people who are sufficiently motivated to write letters about an issue is usually far exceeded by the number of people who are concerned about it. The more letters the company gets concerning an issue, the more attention it is likely to pay to it. Responding to a letter forces the company to develop a considered reaction to the issue raised. For example, if a shareholder writes to ask a company what its environmental policy is, and it does not have one, it must then hold a meeting to draw one up, or to come up with an excuse for not having done so. Letters provide a reason for companies to react; it is not uncommon for companies to make up policy as they go along in this way. A shareholder's letter will often provide a company manager with the opportunity for a formal policy review.

It is possible for individuals to take their activities further by paying close attention to what the company writes in its annual report, and by attending the annual general meeting and asking questions. Attending shareholders' meetings may involve taking time off work and travelling a considerable distance, and it is quite possible that even if a shareholder makes the effort he or she will not be invited to ask a question at the AGM. This level of activity thus involves a more substantial undertaking, although, from the principles of shareholder sovereignty in company law one would expect this to be an action more shareholders would be prepared to engage in.

Because shareholder action is often a time-consuming and costly activity, this handbook has opted to illustrate it by focusing on action taken by groups. It is worth emphasising that this choice has been made for explanatory purposes, not because individual action is ineffective. In fact, a number of carefully targeted individual actions have been very successful in the past; particularly those taken by individuals whose jobs and expertise put them in positions of special influence. While the following pages refer to the activities of groups, many of the kinds of activities discussed are viable options for sufficiently motivated individuals.

Group Activity

Shareholder campaigning groups and coalitions provide an institutional framework for shareholder action that is capable of devoting considerable time to it, and sustaining it over several years. Some of these groupings are loose coalitions of individuals and organisations associating to take collective shareholder action; others are dedicated shareholder action groups with a definite identity and organisation, and sometimes even paid staff. Shareholder groups and coalitions can be characterised in terms of the kinds of objectives they pursue.

1. Single issue groups that pursue just one fairly narrow objective — e.g. campaigns to get companies to withdraw from South Africa.

2. Related issue groups that pursue a range of connected objectives — e.g. groups that aim to improve companies' environmental performance.

Both of these kinds of group may focus on one or more companies. They may not be exclusively shareholder campaigners, but may simply be using shareholder action against companies as one of many tools for pursuing their objectives.

3. Single-company action groups that have open-ended objectives to improve the policy of a single company over the full range of its activities.

4. Industrial sector based groups that have objectives connected to issues specific to an industrial sector — e.g. a group that campaigns on issues related to mining and on mining companies.

5. Pressure groups whose objective is not to campaign on a particular issue or company, but to promote shareholder action as a tool. Their objective is to make shareholder action an effective technique and to help others to use it — e.g. a 'clearing house' on shareholder action.

6. Shareholder protection groups that seek to protect the rights of small shareholders and organise action in order to do so.

7. Institutional investor coalitions that aim to use their collective shareholder voting power to promote a range of more socially responsible business practices.

These categories overlap and are not exhaustive. Shareholder action groups can also be categorised in a number of other ways, for example according to

1. The purpose for which members of the group hold shares — the shares might be an investment first and a tool for shareholder action second, or vice versa.

2. The political perspective held by the shareholder activist — for example a 'revolutionary' approach suggests that modern capitalism is basically bad, and that shareholder militancy can serve as a means to hasten its demise; a reformist one uses shareholder action to push for incremental change within the capitalist system.

3. The premise upon which action is based — is the shareholder taking action because he or she sees it as a right and responsibility of share ownership, or because shareholder action is a means for achieving a particular end?

The objectives, strategy and process of shareholder action that shareholder activists adopt will depend on which of the above categories the shareholders fit into. In practice, the principle divide between existing shareholder activists is that between campaigning groups and investor groups. Campaigning groups are primarily interested in changing the social policies of companies and have little or no explicit interest in the financial performance of the business; investor groups, on the other hand, are primarily concerned about the long-term financial performance while seeing social responsibility issues as important subsidiary questions. The tensions resulting from these differences will be covered in the subsequent section on shareholder action coalitions (see page 106).

Shareholder Action and Pressure

Shareholder action has been used effectively as a tool for getting companies to change their behaviour, particularly in the USA. Where it has been effective, its success has often been achieved by a mixture of dialogue, persuasion and pressure. In many ways shareholder action is not dissimilar to other broader pressure activities, like lobbying government to give more aid to the third world or to ban tobacco advertising.

Getting institutions like governments or companies, and decision-makers within those institutions, to change their minds is rarely easy, but there are a number of skills and techniques that improve the chances of success. Des Wilson (a veteran campaigner who has run campaigns for Shelter, for the Campaign for Lead-free Air, for the freedom of government information, and for the Liberal Democrats at the 1992 general election) has coined the 'three P's' of pressure group activity',[40] in his excellent book *Pressure: The A to Z of Campaigning in Britain*. The 'three P's' are the basic principles that he thinks are essential for successful pressure activity: persistence, professionalism, and perspective.

Persistence

People need time to change. Institutions like companies need even more time. For this reason shareholder action can require several years to be effective. Shareholder activists, therfore, have to take a long term view. For example a fairly typical campaign in the USA, concerning a large American company's operations in the Dominican Republic, took three years of hard campaigning work before any substantial moves were made by the company. Tim Smith, the Director of the Interfaith Center on Corporate Responsibility in the USA, found that when ICCR started taking shareholder action in the early 1970s companies did not consider that social and ethical questions were in any way part of their brief. They believed that their responsibility was limited to looking after the interests of the shareholders. The debate between ICCR and the companies therefore focused on whether or not companies should take ethical questions into consideration at all. However, after a decade's steady pressure, companies began to change their position and the debate moved onto different ground — rather than *whether* they had social responsibilities the discussion became one of *how far* those responsibilities should go.

This does not mean that shareholder activists should not expect any changes for a decade, but it does indicate that large changes happen slowly, but they *do happen*. Therefore shareholder activists need stamina, they need to be prepared to devote a significant amount of their time, and to be prepared for set-backs. Wilson recommends that large scale action should not be undertaken unless it is accompanied by the determination to see the action through to the end. This is, he says, because every failure within a specific area makes a fresh initiative in the same area more difficult — reinforcing the opposition's self-confidence, and belief that there is no need to change. So it is better to start slowly with fairly modest objectives, gradually building up a string of small successes over a few years, than beginning with a hugely ambitious goal that cannot reasonably be realised. Another aspect of persistence Wilson mentions is that campaigning is about meticulous attention to detail. Which means following up every opportunity, every contact; being precise about information, requests, allegations, and demands; being prompt; and keeping meticulous records.

Professionalism

Wilson argues that 'it is the height of irresponsibility to take on a cause that may affect the welfare of others, and then not do it properly . . . If a campaign is incompetently or carelessly run it will be assumed by others to be of no consequence.'[41] This might overstate the case, but it is true that any shareholders' campaign on a company will inform the company's attitude towards the issue concerned and campaigning groups as a whole. A slapdash shareholder action campaign can be more damaging than not doing the campaign at all. While most company public affairs departments realise that campaigning groups are varied and that some are highly professional, individual company directors can very easily have their prejudices about 'activists' confirmed by a sloppy, ill-informed shareholder action campaign. Being professional does not take all that much, in terms of skill, time and money. In fact it can often save both time and money in the long run. What professionalism does require is attention to detail: getting facts right, using good printed material, preparing carefully for all contact with the company, keeping accurate records, answering the telephone properly etc.[42] Another way to enhance the appearance of professionalism is to enlist sympathetic professional people in the campaign — accountants, lawyers and journalists, for example. Many professionals have social concerns but little opportunity to express them, and would welcome the chance to use their skills in interesting and valuable ways.

Perspective

It is vital for shareholder activists to see their concerns in context, both in terms of the world's many other problems and in terms of the company's position and policies. The managements of large international companies face pressure from many different groups with widely diverging and often conflicting interests. So, while an individual shareholder action may well strike a nerve in the company, it is unlikely to be the only nerve which is being stimulated at any one time. The company's policy makers have a range of other priorities. The task for shareholder activists is to try to move their concerns higher up the priority list.

Wilson suggests that without a sense of perspective it possible for someone deeply involved in a campaign to become a fanatic. It is easy to lose sight of what is important and what is not, which produces 'a tendency to paranoia, so that everyone who is even sceptical, let alone arguing the opposite side, is automatically assumed to have sinister motives, and is often criticised and condemned, with no evidence whatsoever, in a way that discredits the campaigners'[43]

Activists should always try to be positive. This means presenting action as being *for* things, rather than against them. So action could be presented as a campaign *for* a more responsible company, rather than a campaign *against* the irresponsible company; for a change in policy rather than against a negative policy. 'It is of importance to hold out the possibility of better circumstances and to define the ultimate objective. The ultimate objective is not out to destroy and defeat but rather to create and improve.'[44] Wilson advises activists to try and see the positive side of the activity they are opposing. Sometimes this is just not possible, but usually there is a positive side — one can appreciate the advantages of cars while trying to minimise their environmental impact. He also argues that from a psychological point of view, long term success is more likely if company representatives are thanked and praised for having taken a step forward, rather than damned for having taken too small a step. The point is to get decision makers into a receptive mood, rather than getting them thinking that even when they begin to concede ground they remain condemned.

Chapter 5
Preparation for Action

The success of shareholder action is to a large extent dependent on its preparation. Preparation involves:

● Researching the issues that are relevant to the campaign.
● Deciding upon realistic objectives.
● Deciding how those objectives should be pursued.
● Working out how and when to present action.
● Developing the appropriate level of organisation to handle the action.
● Raising money to fund action.
● Preparing to deal with the press.
● Building contacts and support.

This section considers these and other key steps in the planning of shareholder action.

Buying Shares

Shares can be bought via stockbrokers, both in the City of London and elsewhere in the UK; via share dealing services run by high-street banks; and by phone or post from organisations like the Share Centre Ltd. The deregulation or the financial services sector during the 1980s has meant that charges for share dealing vary considerably, which makes it worth shopping around. There are four basic components of charges: the price of the share, government stamp duty (0.5% of the share value), the brokers commission, and flat rate additional broking charges. The commission and the flat rate charges are the key variables. Commissions are a small percentage, usually under 2%, of the value of the transaction, they vary depending on the size of deal and the extra services the broker offers. The fixed minimum charge that brokers usually have varies between £10 and £30. At the time of writing examples include The Share Center Ltd, which offers a basic dealing service and charges a 1% commission subject to a minimum of £9.75, and share dealing can be done by phone or post on account, which is the common procedure; Gerrard Vivian Gray Ltd, a City stockbroker, which charges a commission of 1.95% on the first £7,500 together with a 'compliance charge' of £10; and Lloyds Bank, which charges a commission of 1.65% (subject to a minimum of £25) together with an 'administration fee' of £5.

Because of the minimum charges, buying small numbers of shares on the stock market can be expensive. One way of reducing the cost of a large number of small transactions is by transferring of shares between individuals. Shares are property, so their ownership can be transferred. If one person buys, say, 100 shares on the stock market, paying one transaction charge, he or she can then transfer ownership of single shares or groups of shares to a number of other individuals, without involving expensive stockbrokers in the process.

Transferring shares is not without its difficulties. The transfer process is managed by the company, not the stockmarket. The procedure is bureaucratic, taking place by means of an designated transfer form. The form can be bought from legal stationers, and information about the procedure should be obtainable from the company secretary's office. Companies are not generally as quick as the Stock Exchange so the transfer process can take time. Some companies' articles of association allow the directors to refuse to accept a share transfer from taking place, but this restriction should not apply to companies listed on the stock market since it is a stock market requirement for listed companies to allow the free transfer of their shares.[45] The new computerised Taurus share transaction system, currently being introduced, will simplify the share transfer process in the future.

Researching the Issues

It is worth putting effort into research, if only because good information reduces the likelihood of being wrong. Research provides a solid basis of facts and arguments upon which to build action. It helps define the key problems, and so helps clarify what objectives are most worth pursuing. It is advisable to break the process of research down into steps. For example, would-be shareholder activists who already own shares in a company, and who wish to try and make their company more socially responsible, will have a different research approach to people who are concerned about a particular issue and want to use shareholder action as a tool for furthering their cause.

For would-be activists who already own shares in a company, one possible research programme would be:

1. Find out what the company is doing, what kinds of business it is involved in — for example, the company may have interests in agribusiness, and textile manufacture.

Sources: company annual reports, Extel and McCarthy cards, Kompass, Who Owns Whom (see appendix for details).

2. Find out what the key social responsibility issues are concerning those kinds of business — for example, research might uncover a range of specific public concerns about the kinds of agribusiness the company is involved in; as well as concerns about the working conditions in the third world textile factories that many UK textile companies operate.

Sources: pressure groups in specific areas, the media.

3. Find out more about how the company's activities relate to these specific issues — it may turn out that the company obtains only a very small amount of textiles from the third world, and that its agribusiness division is mainly involved with factory farming.

Sources: company annual reports, company divisional reports, company subsidiary reports.

4. Select one or two of the issues of particular interest that the company is involved with to focus on — for example, the company's farming activities.

5. Research the selected issue in depth, breaking it up into various sub-issues — for example, intensive pig farming, battery chicken farming, animal feed quality, the use of growth hormones etc.

Sources: contact with the company, pressure groups, the media, government departments and agencies etc.

6. Focus down to the problems associated with specific company policies and practices, and possible solutions — for example, the transportation over long distance of live pigs and changing policy to minimise this; a policy to phase out battery farming and replace it with free-range chicken rearing.

Once a detailed practical knowledge of a few selected issues has been achieved, the next stage is to develop objectives and strategy.

If, on the other hand, would-be shareholder activists do not own shares in a particular company, but are interested instead in a particular set of issues, an alternative research programme could be:

a. Define which of the issues of concern are particularly related to British companies — for example, if the prospective activists are interested in third world issues, the debt crisis, the arms trade, and the working conditions and environmental policy of companies operating overseas are all issues relevant to British companies, but famine, human rights abuses and tariff barriers may not be.

b. Select just one or two of these issues, and research them in more detail, focusing on how they relate specifically to company activities.

c. Find out which big UK companies are involved with the issues of concern.

d. Select from among these, one or two companies that look likely to be the best candidates for shareholder action — this may involve questions like how sensitive are the companies likely to be to adverse publicity, how big their third world operations are, and their comparative records.

e. Focus on the problems associated with specific company policies and practices, and possible solutions.

For almost any issue prospective activists choose to take shareholder action on, there are bound to be people in Britain paid to be experts on that issue who will be happy to discuss it. Most controversial issues are controversial precisely because 'experts' in pressure groups, research institutes, parliament, business or the media are persistently fighting for their side of the argument. So there are invariably people prepared to supply information on issues, and help with research, although this help is often biased. (It is therefore worth trying to work out what interests are motivating those providing information.) Sources of information on issues and companies are listed in the appendix.

Selecting the issues and the companies to take action involves a number of considerations. In the case of issues:

● Is the issue timely?

● Is it being reported by the press?

- Are there any pressure group campaigns, or parliamentary and EC activity expected to take place in the coming year that will attract attention to it?

- Are other companies publicly improving their policy on the issue?

- Is there an opportunity for good public relations for the company on the issue?

- Is the issue long term or short term? (For example, it may not be worthwhile starting up action to get a company to voluntarily limit its transportation of live animals if new legislation is planned that will force it to do so anyway).

- Will the bulk of the general public be supportive or is the issue a minority concern?

- Is this issue simple or is it very complicated?

- Is there agreement among most of 'the experts', or trenchant disagreement?

Choosing companies to campaign on is difficult. It is hard to know in advance which companies are going to prove receptive to persuasion, and which will resist it. Generally speaking the companies that are most likely to respond positively to shareholder action are companies that have already demonstrated a concern about social responsibility issues, and those companies which are particularly sensitive to public opinion. The best way to find these things out is to ask people who are experienced in dealing with companies. Organisations like New Consumer, EIRIS, and CEP in the USA have dealt with hundreds of large companies; some of the larger pressure groups have also had dealings with specific companies. It is possible to get a rough idea of how sensitive to public opinion a company is likely to be by considering:

- Whether the company sells its goods or services directly to the public.

- Whether the company advertises widely in the media.

- Whether it has a strong public reputation.

- Whether it retails under its own name, or is concealed behind brand names.

- Whether the company has had trouble in the past because of campaigns on it.

- Whether its annual report makes extensive reference to its public spiritedness.

- How generous its corporate giving is.

One can get an indication of a company's interest in social issues by finding out:

- Whether the company has designated a special post in the PR department to deal with environmental or social responsibility issues.

- Whether the company makes significant reference to these issues in its annual report.

- What material on social responsibility issues the company has prepared

- What written policies it has on social issues.

None of these points are conclusive indications of a company's likely receptivity to shareholders on social responsibility issues; they only provide a very rough guide. In any case, there are good reasons for not choosing the most receptive companies to campaign on: if a company is insensitive to public opinion it may make shareholder action more difficult, but it makes it more necessary.

In order to undertake substantial shareholder action on companies it is essential to build up a basic expertise on the specific issues that provide the focus for action. It is not necessary to understand all the finer technical details, but it is essential to have a working knowledge of what the main arguments, problems and proposed solutions are, as well as a basic grasp of the relevant facts. This is what makes narrowing the area of research down to just a couple of specific issues so important. To get a broad expertise over a whole set of issues takes an enormous amount of time and effort. Selecting and prioritising the issues for research is therefore the only viable way of proceeding. In any case, the most effective campaigns tend to only focus on one issue at any one time. So there is no particular advantage in devoting large amounts of time to mastering issues that will not be the object of action in the immediate future.

Objectives

Once the background research is complete, a clear picture of the specific problems of the particular policies of individual companies should emerge. A fairly clear idea of the solutions to these problems should begin to appear as well. Once this position has been reached, work can begin on selecting the objectives to be worked towards. It is worth deciding both what would be the ideal goals of the shareholder action campaign, and what the realistic objectives are. This provides both the sense of a long term ambition that can be aimed at, as well as a concrete, short or medium term goal that can be worked for. It is important to keep the short term objectives low enough to be achievable. Campaigners who set their sights too high spend years without achieving any solid goals at all, and so lack the feeling that they are getting somewhere. Rather than having one single monolithic objective, it is important to break it into a number of more specific ones. This allows successes to be added one by one, gradually building a solid base of achievement upon which to proceed. Breaking objectives up also makes planning action much easier.

The specific objectives of shareholder action will primarily be to achieve practical changes in company policy or behaviour. The most achievable objectives are those that the company can implement without inordinate difficulty or cost, and that require a straightforward, definite decision to be made by the company directors. A broad objective to, say, change the company's attitude to environmental issues may, if achieved, be at least as valuable in the long term as a specific policy change. But as a goal for shareholder action such a broad objective is unmanageable, and so does not offer a solid base for action. Concrete policy objectives are therefore better than general ones. It is important to write the objectives down clearly and precisely, so there is always an exact record to refer back to. Objectives have a surprising tendency to be forgotten, or to mutate into something quite different. Finally, objectives should be a tool for action, not a cage for it; if compelling reasons emerge for replacing or revising objectives they should not be ignored.

It may be helpful to give an example illustrating the selection of objectives. Imagine a shareholders action group that is concerned about the lack of representation of ethnic minority members in big companies. The group does some background research and discovers that, while 15% of young whites were unemployed in the late 1980s, the figures were 28% for young Afro-Caribbeans, 22% for young Indians and 31% for Bangladeshis and Pakistanis, suggesting that there may still be a significant level of racial discrimination in the employment practices of British companies which, despite plenty of goodwill from companies, is proving remarkably persistent. The group also discovers that while many companies have equal opportunities policies, they tend not to be implemented very effectively, and that many companies do not monitor the numbers and position of ethnic minorities who work for them, so they have no data from which to tackle the problem.[46] The group's long-term, ideal goal could be:

> Members of ethnic minorities should be represented at all levels of the company in the same proportion as they are found in the communities in which the company operates.

In most companies this aim would be ambitious, but not impossible to achieve in the long term. Once it has established this goal, the group then needs to decide upon concrete objectives that will help towards achieving it. Further research, and discussion with other interested parties might suggest they could be:

1. The company should have a detailed equal opportunities policy, with a plan for implementing it.

2. The company should monitor the ethnic origin of its employees.

These objectives give a clearer idea of what the group wants the company to do, but they are still rather vague. What counts as a detailed equal opportunities policy? Or a plan for implementing it? What form should the monitoring take? How will the group know whether, once the company adopts the policy, it will actively pursue it? These are important questions, the answers to which can make the difference between a productive policy and corporate public relations window-dressing. If a company does not already have an equal opportunities policy it might not be too hard to get it to adopt one, but if the group does not specify what the policy should address then the company can get away with high-minded rhetoric, good for public relations but masking the fact that the company is doing virtually nothing about equal opportunities. So the group's objectives should be as specific as possible. For example:

1. The company should appoint an executive with responsibility for the equal opportunities programme.

2. The company should adopt an equal opportunities policy, drawn up in consultation with the Commission on Racial Equality. As a minimum it should specify procedures and training for ensuring:

a. Jobs are advertised widely including in the ethnic minority press.

b. The recruitment, selection and promotion procedures are not biased against ethnic groups.

c. Jobs should be advertised and interviewees assessed on the basis of the qualities needed for the job, not on the basis of other superfluous qualifications, that members of ethnic minorities might not have access to.

3. The company should monitor and record the ethnicity of all applicants for jobs and for promotion within the company, and of the successful candidates. The company should publish a summary of this information in the annual report to shareholders.

4. The company should set targets for increasing ethnic minority representation where it is lacking, and develop strategies for meeting them. It should publish a summary of these.

5. The company should institute training programmes that enable ethnic minorities to become qualified for promotion.

This list of objectives is by no means exhaustive, but is already well beyond what can probably be achieved in a single shareholder action campaign. So the objectives need to be ranked in order of priority. Perhaps 1, 2 and 3 should be the first stage of objectives, and, if successful, 4 and 5 can be added as further objectives.

Strategy

Once the objectives have been defined, decisions must be made about how to pursue them. In shareholder action, the achievement of an objective usually entails the need for a policy decision to be taken by someone, or some people, in the company. One of the crucial stages in the process of planning action, is to work out the route towards this decision.[47] And this means finding out:

● Who takes the decision?

● Who is involved in the decision-making process?

● What factors influence the process?

● What kinds of persuasion or pressure need to be applied to the decision makers?

● Where are the points most vulnerable to pressure?

Decisions to change company policy are usually made by a company's executive directors. The route to a decision of this kind is complicated. Contrary to the simple economic theory, company policy is rarely decided by the directors sitting down together and rationally working out the course of action that would lead to the highest profits for the company. In practice there are other considerations. To take one example, corporate decision-making can be affected as much by the individual managers' desire for power, prestige, job security and a high income as by the company's long term profitability. These kinds of considerations may, for example, lead managers to expand the size or influence of their departments or the company as a whole, rather than aiming to increase its profitability; or alternatively it may lead them to minimise risk and change, rather than adapting to market conditions in an optimal manner.

When a company changes, it does so for a variety of often complex reasons; not merely because the shareholders want it to, or because the board thinks the change is going to boost profits, or because it is the ethically correct thing to do. As the publicity director of Iceland Frozen Foods has said about her company's conversion to environmental friendliness in a speech to Business in the Community,

> Why do we want to be green? It's fashionable. It's a good thing to write in the annual report. It gets the pressure groups off your back. It's a good publicity getter. That may be the cynic's view, but I have to say there's a lot of truth to it too. But there's more to it than that. If we're honest that's the way most companies get into it but it gathers its own momentum and many other advantages unfold.[48]

This indicates the range of factors influencing corporate decision-making. These factors are represented by a large number of individuals and interest groups both inside and outside the company. Inside the company there are a range of specialist policy-makers such as its public relations, marketing, financial, production and personnel managers. These individuals have their own personal objectives and interests, but they are also representatives for a range of interest groups operating within companies. These are based upon different company divisions and different company functions, such as business development, personnel, information technology, accounts, sales and marketing, production, general management etc. These interest groups each have various requirements and goals. Outside the company there are a further range of individuals and organisations that can have influence in the decision-making process. These include large institutional fund managers, professional consultants, regulators, politicians, influential financial journalists and newspapers, the directors' peer group, their personal acquaintances, including their families, as well as consumer, employee and producer groups, and public opinion as a whole.

The key point is that companies are not the monolithic entities that they appear to be. The are divided by differences of opinion and interest. Sophisticated shareholder activists will be able to make use of these divisions, forming tacit alliances with those in the company whose interests favour the reforms they are proposing. For example, the staff of the environmental unit of a company may genuinely wish to see a much stronger company environmental policy, while the production managers do not. The environmental unit may be able to use the pressure supplied by shareholder activists to convince the board to back them.

The range of the interests which these individuals and groups have is large, and varies from company to company and from year to year. Getting a feel for the way interests and power currently operate within the individual company that is the object of action is therefore as difficult as it is important. Reading press articles on the company, and the company's own literature begins to generate an impression. Talking to other groups and individuals who have been involved with the company in the past, such as other campaigning groups and other shareholders, can broaden the picture. Ultimately a fuller understanding can only really be gleaned as the shareholder action campaign gets under way and the activists deal with members of the company directly. The way the company responds to the campaign provides the best indication about the public relations department's attitude, and indirectly about the general posture of the company. Meeting with representatives of the company privately to discuss the issues can provide an even clearer picture of the situation. It is, however, impossible to get a full, complete picture. Only the most astute of the people actually *working for* the company will have a fair idea, and even this will be limited in various ways. Nevertheless, the better activists can understand the factors influencing decision-making, the more likely any action taken will be effective.

Chapter 6
Targets for Shareholder Action

Once a shareholder action campaign becomes established, it is easier to get a feel for how a company's decision-making process works, and for the identity of the key people or groups that affect it. Once this begins to happen it is useful to start to compile a list of the key targets for persuasion. The list can be accompanied by details of how each target fits into a company's decision-making structure, and how each target might be used to further the campaign objectives. This kind of list is open to continuous revision as knowledge of the company increases, and as individuals targeted prove more, or less, useful than others.

Not all targets can or should be approached directly. For example, many companies object to outsiders approaching employees directly on sensitive issues. They prefer everything to be handled by the public relations department. This is not to say that activists should not try — it can happen that a company employee, say a production manager, can reveal in a couple of unguarded minutes on the telephone what the public relations department has been energetically concealing from the activists. This approach is risky, however, because the PR department will not be pleased if they find out, and so it could sour relations with them.

Planning how to approach targets, and in what order, is one of the most important single areas of a shareholder action campaign. For example, once the directors are forced to take a stand actively against a shareholder group's activities, they can bring enormous resources into play — money, the corporate bureaucracy, the company's lawyers, public relations advisors, accountants and management consultants — to find ways to protect and defend the directors' position. If a shareholder action campaign starts off by being unnecessarily aggressive or negative, it risks setting this formidable public relations machine in motion from the start, making the task significantly harder. The people who are the targets for shareholder action have to be treated very intelligently. Irritate or embarrass them without good reason and the task becomes twice as hard.

Targets for shareholder action include the following:

Inside the company
- The chairman
- The chief executive
- The executive directors
- The non-executive directors
- The board as a whole
- The company secretary's office
- The public relations department
- Other company departments (e.g. marketing or personnel)
- Subsidiaries of the parent company and vice versa
- The employees of the company

Outside the company
- Trading partners of the company (e.g. banks or suppliers)
- The consumers of the company's products
- Advisors to the company (e.g. PR or environmental advisors)
- Acquaintances of decision makers (e.g. peer group)
- Professional bodies (e.g. the Institute of Directors)
- Institutional shareholders and fund managers
- Stockbrokers and company analysts
- Small shareholders
- Trade unions
- Regulators
- Central government
- Local government
- Local community groups
- Pressure groups
- The financial press
- The mainstream press
- Television and radio

For each target group selected, shareholder activists should have named individuals or groups which will be the specific targets for action. It is not productive to try and tackle all of these targets at the same time, in fact it will often be counterproductive. For example, if a frank dialogue is in progress, privately, with representatives of a company, getting an article about the campaign on the company into the national press is likely to lead to the conversation with the company becoming markedly less frank.

The central group of targets for shareholder action is the senior management and executive personnel within the company. The central targets are in turn influenced by other secondary targets. The most significant of these are the institutional shareholders and the press. The discussion so far concerning targets for action has covered the main points about targets inside the company. We now turn to the key subsidiary targets.

Institutional Investors

Institutional investors own the bulk of the shares in British companies; they are increasingly inclined to use this influence in a positive way. This makes institutional investors, together with the press, the most important secondary targets of any shareholder action campaign. Institutional investors own such large volumes of shares that companies listen to them as a matter of course. If shareholder activists can persuade institutional investors to support their cause, they gain considerable advantage.

Institutional investors include insurance companies, pension funds, church funds, union funds, local authority funds and also the fund managers who manage investments for other people. They now account for around two-thirds of shares held in large British companies. Big institutions, like Prudential Corporation PLC, own several percent of the shares in a number of Britain's largest companies. British pension funds control a third of the shares in British industry, worth over £250bn, and, as Anne Simpson of PIRC has said, they are thus 'responsible for whole swathes of the British economy, for good or ill, their successes and failures effect us all.'[50] In the past, institutional investors have been very passive in their share ownership, rarely interfering with company management. It used to be the case that if an institution was unhappy with a company's performance it would sell its shares — in America this is known as the Wall Street Walk — but now individual institutions own such large chunks of shares in individual companies that it has become hard for them to sell their shares without adversely affecting the share price, and thus the value of the shares they are trying to dispose of. Consequently, institutions are becoming more ready to take an interest in the long term profitability of companies and so in the quality of corporate management and company policy. This is making them more interventionist. In Britain this intervention largely takes place behind closed doors, which has tended to mean a quiet word over dinner with a company director.

Recently, large institutional investors have become a bit more aggressive. Norwich Union, a large insurance company, is reported to summon representatives of two of the companies in which it holds investments to its offices each week, where it interrogates them about their companies' performance and policy. Norwich Union also has a policy document setting out what action it should regularly take as a major shareholder, and employs twelve researchers to help its fund managers monitor investments. There were no researchers five years ago.[51] The Institutional Fund Managers Association has recommended that institutional investors should at least bother to cast their votes at annual general meetings — the practice in the past has commonly been to avoid voting. Other industry bodies like the Association of British Insurers and the Institutional Shareholders Committee have set out guidelines for best practice for directors, with the implication that, if these are not met, institutional investors should take action. There is growing support for the opinion that institutional investors should take a more active role in corporate governance.

In the USA this process began taking place a decade ago. Now, a broad spectrum of institutional investors take regular shareholder action with the companies they invest in. The most significant activist institutions are the public employees' pension funds, which have a total of $700bn of investments. Calpers, the California state pension fund, is the biggest fund in America with investments of $68bn. In 1992 it took action on directors' pay, independent directors, and other issues with twelve companies, nine of which promised to change their policies as a result.[52] The five New York City public employee pension funds, with a total of $42bn, invested on behalf of 530,000 employees, are even more activist. The New York State pension funds own shares in a total of 2,300 companies. They hold their shares in each company for an average of twelve years, making them interested in long term issues. In 1991 the New York funds filed over two dozen resolutions, with varying success. One of their more successful resolutions was put to the 1991 AGM of Harcourt Brace Jovanovitch, a large publishing company. Harcourt was performing badly. One of the controllers of the New York funds suspected that part of the problem was that there were no properly independent directors on the board, and so filed a resolution that the board appoint independent directors to more than half of its board positions. The resolution received an impressive 34.5% of the vote in its favour.

In the USA as a whole, over 300 social responsibility resolutions were filed by pension funds, church investors, and other groups and individuals in 1992, together with well over 100 on corporate governance issues like directors' pay and independent directors. A large proportion of the church based institutions are members of the Interfaith Center for Corporate Responsibility. ICCR is a New York based clearing house for shareholder action by church groups which was set up in 1971, it has over 250 Protestant and Roman Catholic institutional members, including national church denomination and agencies, religious communities, dioceses, pension funds and health care corporations. There are several other organisations in the USA and Canada which coordinate American action. These include the Taskforce on the Churches and Corporate Responsibility (TCCR) in Canada; the United Shareholders Association (USA) for small shareholders; and the Council on Economic Priorities (CEP) on general corporate responsibility issues.

The movement for activist institutional investor involvement is beginning to make itself felt on this side of the Atlantic. In 1991 the South Yorkshire Pensions Authority, together with local authority funds from Derbyshire, Lancashire, Cleveland, Humberside and Lewisham, and one private sector fund, attempted to bring a resolution to the Fisons PLC AGM, calling for the company to stop its peat-cutting operations in ecologically sensitive areas. Unfortunately, the coalition of funds failed to meet the full requirements for submission of resolutions by the deadline.

The Fisons action was coordinated by Pensions and Investments Research Consultants Ltd (PIRC). PIRC is an independent company, set up by a consortium of pension funds as an independent agency to provide research, advice and coordination between shareholders. Currently, twelve public sector pension funds subscribe to PIRC's services, representing investments totalling £14bn. PIRC coordinates a range of shareholder activities on behalf of these investors. PIRC also has an agreement with the Washington-based Investor Responsibility Research Center (IRRC), which allows the swapping of infomation on trans-Atlantic shareholder action. Due to the internationalisation of global stockmarkets, many large American institutional investors own shares in British companies and want to vote with them, as they are legally obliged to do so for their US shares. This means that many American investors may be in a position to help with resolutions proposed by British shareholder activists. IRRC's Global Shareholder Consortium of over 30 US institutions had over $5bn of shares in British companies in 1992.

While PIRC is the main centre for institutional shareholder activity in Britain, there are signs that the activity is spreading. In 1988 the Ecumenical Committee on Corporate Responsibility was founded to coordinate the churches' work on corporate responsibility in Britain, as ICCR does in the USA. So far, ECCR has produced a number of reports and plans to coordinate church action on equal opportunities for ethnic minorities in the near future.

Shareholder activists who are able to enlist the support of one or more institutional investor will have considerable advantages. The support of an institutional investor adds substantial weight to a campaign. Both the press and the company concerned will take campaigns supported by institutional investors much more seriously than those supported by a number of tiny shareholders. The support of an institution also has practical advantages, including the possibility of financial aid, legal advice and further contacts. While many institutional investors are increasingly keen to take shareholder action, they need to be persuaded to participate. The principles for persuading institutional investors to do this are the same kind as those required for persuading company decision makers to change their minds. Institutional investors are targets who have to take a decision about whether to support an activity or not. Working out the best way to achieve this objective requires research into the institution's structure:

- Who are its trustees?
- What are their backgrounds?
- Which fund manager manages the institution's investments?
- What is its record on shareholder action?

- Who are the beneficiaries of the institution?
- Can they be persuaded to put pressure on the trustees?

Success in persuading an institution to lend its support also demands a clear idea of precisely what is needed from the institution. While it would be desirable to get an institution to give its 'general support', institutions tend to want to know, in the clearest terms, what they are letting themselves in for. Institutions should therefore be approached carefully with a negotiable, but otherwise definite, plan of campaign, specifying a demarcated activity that they are requested to perform. One of the key reasons for care to be taken is that most institutions are very careful about the kind of publicity they get. They are very reluctant to commit themselves to campaigns where they do not know precisely what risks they are taking. The appearance of professionalism is particularly important when courting institutional investors. Perhaps the best first step is to contact one of the organisations mentioned above, particularly PIRC in Britain, and ask for advice on how to proceed.

Company Analysts

Another key target group for shareholder action is the company analysts employed by the large City stockbroking companies. Company analysts provide the City with expert opinions about company performance, and forecasts of future performance. They decide whether a given company's shares are over-priced or under-priced, providing the markets with advice about whether to buy, sell, or hold the shares of particular companies. If shareholder activists can persuade company analysts that a company is failing to address an issue that is important to its future prospects, then this action could have serious repercussions for the company's share price and its future ability to raise capital.

In order to do this, shareholders need to approach analysts with clear, concise well documented arguments that show good grounds for questioning current company policy and strategy. Big brokerage houses employ a large number of company analysts, each specialising in six or seven companies in a given industrial sector (fewer if there are any very large companies in the sector). Analysts often know as much about the insides of 'their' companies as do the companies' own directors, but unlike the directors they are free to publicly criticise companies, which often leads to friction between companies and analysts.

If shareholder activists can break into the analysis process, their intervention can have a marked long-term impact. The sorts of elements that go into an analyst's assessment of a company are:

- The company's contracts.
- The state of its markets and its market position.
- The viability of its strategy.
- The quality of its management.
- The quality of its technology.
- The accuracy of its accounts.
- The company's projected earnings figures.

Analysts get the bulk of their information about these things from companies, not from outside groups. If outside groups, like shareholder activists, are able to provide quality information about companies, analysts are alikely to welcome it. If the information convinces an analyst to change his or her judgement of a company, the analyst will circulate the new opinion, effectively leading to the analyst serving as a tacit advocate for the shareholder activists' cause.

In order to mount effective action on this target group, campaigners need to identify the key City analysts for each company, and to supply them regularly with information about the campaign, focusing on the negative financial consequences of the company's failure to address the campaigners' key issues. Shareholder activists should also try to get hold of the analysts' reports on companies, providing a critical feedback to the analyst — when for example, an analyst fails to take future environmental and social costs into account while estimating the profit due to a new investment project.

This kind of shareholder action has not been very common in Britain, although the scale of activity does seem to be increasing. In April 1992, Surfers Against Sewage made a presentation at James Capel, a large City broker, concerning the environmental performance of South West Water PLC. The presentation was attended by a number of institutional investors and fund managers, including AMP Pearl, Ecclesiastical Insurance, Friends Provident, John Govett, Henderson Administration, Jupiter Tyndall, and JC Investment Management. The presentation highlighted, in some detail, several areas in which South West Water's sewage management strategy was alleged to be damaging to the company's financial prospects. According to the chairman of SAS, the meeting was instrumental in provoking South West Water into setting up an Environmental Forum. The Forum contains representatives of the company and of SAS, and will meet regularly to discuss the environmental impact of any company investment plan.

Regulators

Another useful target for shareholder activists is industry regulators, such as the National Rivers Authority, OFFGAS, OFFELEC, OFFWAT, HM Inspectorate of Pollution, and local authority planning departments. One example is a recent action on Severn Trent PLC by the four-person Clean Rivers Campaign. The campaign managed to convince the National Rivers Authority that the pollution consent level for a number of the company's sewage plants needed to be upgraded. Following the imposition of higher standards, Severn Trent has had to invest considerable sums in addition to that which it said it would spend in its privatisation prospectus.

Indirect Share Ownership

As mentioned in the introduction to this book, most adults in Britain have a financial interest in shares, without owning them directly themselves. The two most significant sources of individuals' financial interest are in their pensions and insurance premiums. There is considerable scope for people who indirectly control shares in this way to put pressure on pension funds and insurance companies to make more positive use of their shares. The relationships, on the one hand between individuals who hold pensions and their pension fund, and on the other between insurance customers and their insurance company, are different and require different kinds of pressure. In the latter case the relationship is one of buyer and seller. When people buy insurance they enter into a contractual relationship defined by the insurance policy. The insurance company's investment funds (into which it puts premiums, and out of which it pays claims) is entirely separate from the customer. It is up to the insurance company to manage its funds as it sees fit. So there is no right in law for insurance customers to demand that their insurance company uses its funds to take shareholder action. However, because the relationship is one between buyer and seller, traditional forms of consumer pressure can be brought to bear. Insurance companies need customers; if customers want their insurance company to use its funds actively to promote better corporate governance, then it is in the interests of the insurance company to meet this consumer preference. Indeed one insurance company, the Norwich Union, sees the value of pursuing shareholder action, and has built up a research department to do so. If insurance consumers make loud demands to insurers on these matters, the shift towards institutional activism could be encouraged.

The legal relationship between pension holders and their pension fund is somewhat closer than that between insurers and their customers. Pension holders are legal beneficiaries of the pension fund. The pension fund's trustees have a fiduciary duty to manage the fund in a manner likely to be in the long term benefit of their beneficiaries. In the past, the law has been interpreted very narrowly — the long term benefit to the beneficiaries has been seen in restricted financial terms, so trustees have been able to insist that they have no responsibility to involve themselves in shareholder action.

Action inevitably costs money, the beneficiaries' money, so the trustees can argue that taking action is not in the financial interests of the beneficiaries. This book lacks the space for a survey of the present state of pension law, but the law seems to be moving away from its previous restrictive interpretation, to one that allows trustees more leeway to pursue the longer term interests of their beneficiaries in a more intelligent and enlightened manner. In the present climate, it is increasingly worthwhile for pension holders to contact their trustees and make clear what *they* perceive to be in their long term interest, encouraging the trustees to take action on their behalf. It would be even more valuable for pension holders to apply more organised pressure to their trustees, much in the same way that this book encourages shareholders to take action on their directors. It is, after all, the pension holders' money that is invested in the pension fund, so it is reasonable that the pension holder should have a say over how his or her investments are used.

There are good reasons for expecting this sort of indirect shareholder action to be more effective in the long term than direct shareholder action by small shareholders. If even a small proportion of the pension fund sector is persuaded by its beneficiaries to take regular shareholder action on governance and social responsibility issues, the consequences will be felt powerfully throughout industry. The point is that pension funds have the size and organisation to put persistent, heavy pressure on companies in a way that fragmented and sporadic small shareholder action campaigns cannot.

The Ethical Investment Movement

Another form of investment institution that should be mentioned in the context of shareholder action is the growing ethical investment movement. In the past, this movement has been based around the principle of 'negative screening', whereby prospective investments are screened against involvement in a range of ethically controversial issues. This has led to a plethora of investment vehicles, mainly based on unit trusts, which only invest in companies which have no appreciable involvement in areas like South Africa, the arms trade, or heavily polluting industries. These ethically 'clean' funds have attracted some £200m of investment. In addition to the ethical unit trusts, many other large institutions, with far greater investments, have adopted an informal negative screening approach, selling their shares in the more 'questionable' companies. While negative screening is attractive to investors who wish to avoid involvement in companies with 'unsound' business operations, it is not clear that negative screening has any direct value in promoting concrete improvements in corporate practice.

One theoretical aim of negative screening is to deprive 'bad' companies of investment capital, and so putting pressure on them to cease their unethical practices. In reality, as the overwhelming majority of global investment capital is not screened, few 'bad' companies have any trouble attracting the investment they need. In any case, the bulk of capital used by companies for real industrial investment is ultimately in the form of retained company profits and not share capital provided by investors. Negative screening bears resemblance to the boycott principle: if you do not like what a company is doing, hurt it by refusing to buy its products. Boycotts only work if they are public, and if the company fears that it will be losing business as a result. In the case of negative screening, the screened companies are not hurt in any way. The quiet departure of a few small ethical investors does not cost them anything. They are still able to attract more than enough capital to continue their business.

The principle underlying this book is that, in order to change companies' policies, intelligent, carefully planned and organised pressure must be brought to bear on companies over a period of time, often publicly. According to this principle, negative screening is not likely to be much use, and furthermore it can make the work of shareholder activists harder. Those individuals and institutions sufficiently concerned about ethical issues to pay for the negative screening of their investments, are precisely the people who could be involved in positive shareholder action in the companies in which they invest. However, instead of taking their ethical concerns up with the directors, or taking other kinds of shareholder action, negative screening encourages these ethically motivated people to silently sell their shares and move to a 'clean' company, with little practical impact except, inappropriately, a clearer conscience for the investor. There is a real problem that once investors sell their shares in a 'bad' company they lose all interest and influence in it. The more ethically motivated investors that adopt negative screening, the fewer there are left with investments in 'bad' companies to take shareholder action on them.

Fortunately, there are the beginnings of a change in the ethical investment movement, and the reliance on negative screening is being accompanied by positive investment in 'alternative' projects that have social benefit but fail to attract the necessary capital from conventional sources.[53] A more significant change is the acknowledgment that even companies that survive the screening process can benefit from shareholder action, and that screened investment funds should participate in taking this action. The environmental funds managed by Jupiter Tyndall Merlin (JTM), while employing some negative screening, also employ a form of shareholder action known as 'constructive dialogue.' Constructive dialogue involves JTM in active discussion and debate with many of the companies it invests in. This is managed by the environmental research unit which analyses companies for JTM's green funds (including the The Merlin Jupiter Ecology Fund, The Merlin International Green Investment Trust, and funds that JTM manages for other people, including the Citibank Life Green Fund and the Skandia Ethical Selection Fund). JTM is part of a mainstream investment house; the green funds form only a very small proportion of the total funds under Jupiter Tyndall management. The JTM environmental unit has been able to extend its constructive dialogue approach to the much wider range of un-screened companies not represented in its green funds, but represented in Jupiter Tyndall's other mainstream funds.

One logical inference that could be drawn from the argument of this section is the need for a novel alternative form of ethical investment fund which, instead of disinvesting in 'bad' companies, actively chooses to invest in companies with a poor ethical and social performance in order to wage energetic shareholder action campaigns for reform — an ethical investment fund for shareholder action. However, the more concilliatory constructive dialogue approach seems to be the best available option at present. This requires mainstream and ethical investment funds to set up and finance environmental and social responsibility research units to pursue dialogue with companies; something few have done so far.

Other organisations involved in the ethical investment movement include: the Christian Ethical Investment Group which advises churches on investment strategy, and is currectly examining how the churches might move on from a solely negative screening approach; The Independent Shareholders Group, recently established to give small shareholders a stronger voice; the Social Investment Forum which acts as a focal point for debate over socially responsible investment in the UK; and the Ethical Investment Research Service Ltd (EIRIS), a research organisation devoted to screening company activities.

The Media

Gaining publicity for shareholder action has many uses. It can be a very effective way of putting pressure on targets within the company, particularly the public relations department and the directors. However, it does have its drawbacks. Press coverage of shareholder action can rapidly lead to a breakdown in the activists' relationship with the company. This is tolerable if other forms of activity are not working, but if other less confrontational forms of activity have not been tried, it can prevent any chance of cooperative dialogue or negotiation with the company. If handled badly, attempts to get press coverage can lead to a complete stand-off between the two sides, raising the stakes considerably, making it hard for the company to concede anything publicly without some degree of humiliation.

There is little advantage to be gained from getting press coverage for its own sake. Generally speaking, the point of getting press coverage is to put pressure on the various target individuals or groups that have been selected. This usually means that, rather than using just any strategy to get publicity, shareholder activists should only use tactics which are likely to lead to coverage that will further their objectives. Early on in the process of action, while the company may still be cooperative, it is often desirable to avoid press coverage altogether. If the press are interested it is better to try and keep their coverage well informed and reasonable, and to avoid sensationalism. Publicity material should reflect this. Managing the news in this way is never entirely possible, but there are a number of things that can be done to improve the chance of success.

Newspapers are businesses; they will be only too happy to help publicise shareholder activities if there is something in it for them. This something is usually a good story or, even better, a good *exclusive* story. If there is not much in it for them, or if obtaining a story requires too much work, then they will not be so happy to help. Broadly speaking, shareholder activists, and pressure groups more generally, are useful to the media because they are the source of good news stories. However, journalists will rarely come looking, and many prefer to be spoon fed with pre-digested stories, than have to do all the work finding and developing the story themselves. As the media are businesses, it is necessary to be business-like, that is to say flexible, efficient and reliable.

Press Contacts

One of the first priorities of any campaign involving the media is to build up a list of contact names and addresses of journalists. This can be divided into two categories, a broad list of journalists and others who need to be kept informed about shareholder activities, and a more select list of journalists to be nurtured as personal contacts. If, for example, a group of shareholder activists is mounting a campaign that concerns environmental issues, the first list should contain all the environmental correspondents of all the major national newspapers, as well as the BBC and ITN news-desks; the names and addresses of the press officers of the various environmental pressure groups and specialist environmental magazines; and the names of the key financial columnists who cover companies and shares. The second list should include a relatively small number of targeted journalists with whom the group aims to make personal contact. For the activist group in the previous example, this list may well include some of the environmental correspondents of the daily and Sunday newspapers, as well as some of their key financial journalists. These journalists should be chosen carefully, by reading the papers for a few weeks to see who writes about what and with what slant. It is likely that this small group of journalists will be the main source of media coverage, so they should be treated well: used sparingly; kept up-to-date, but only with important developments; fed with exclusives every now and then; and treated with maximum professionalism.

Initially, the target journalists on the second list can be approached with a telephone call telling them about the shareholder action campaign, its objectives, and the main obstacles to its success. If, over a period of time, they are fed with high quality material that they are able to use, they may become invaluable support to the shareholder campaign. Looking after these journalists should therefore be a high priority.

One of the best ways of using these journalists is to offer them feature articles covering the campaign, rather than just news stories. The media have an insatiable appetite for good feature stories. In order to encourage journalists to feature a shareholder campaign, activists should work out how the information to be used could be presented as an interesting and original story. This shows the journalist the potential for the story and saves him or her having to do all the hard imaginative work.

It should be remembered though, that giving good stories to friendly journalists is not a certain way of gaining coverage. All journalists depend, to varying degrees, on their editors for the publication of their work. There is little that can be done to influence this part of the process. Editors are not only concerned about the quality of stories, but with the financial performance of their newspaper. This creates a problem for shareholder action. Newspapers rely heavily on advertising for their income. Shareholder action commonly concerns companies that spend millions of pounds on advertising each year. It is therefore not unreasonable for an editor to want to avoid offending his big advertising clients by publishing stories about them that are critical of their corporate ethics. This means that shareholder action stories may be 'spiked' (withheld from publication) by the editor more frequently than other less advertising-sensitive stories.

Press Releases

Press releases are the standard way of informing the media about events. They tend to be misused by many campaigners. Press releases should be used economically, only when there is something genuinely newsworthy to say. They should be presented very carefully in clear, simple prose. They should contain the basis of a good story, and it should be immediately obvious what is newsworthy about the press release. They should be short. All the basic facts should be in the first paragraph. For example, the first paragraph of a press release about a resolution to be put to an AGM should include: what the resolution is (a brief, simple statement), who is proposing it, where the AGM is taking place, when, and why the resolution is to be proposed. Press releases should be predominantly factual, rather than opinions. Any opinion that is given should be quotable, well worded, able to stand on its own, and accompanied by the name of the person whose opinion it is — your name if it is your opinion. If a press release is particularly time-sensitive, it can be 'embargoed'. If 'Embargoed until Midnight of July 17' is written at the top corner, then journalists should not go public with it until then. Press releases should ideally be on headed notepaper with 'Press Release' written on them. They should be word-processed or typed, with double-spaced lines and wide margins. If a shareholder campaign develops a reputation over time for sending out high-quality press releases, journalists will tend to pay more attention to its press releases than to the mass of others that they get, and so are more likely to follow then up than throw them away.

Sometimes photographic coverage of shareholder activities is easier to obtain than a written news report. Often newspapers will send photographers to events rather than journalists, in which case pictures are the only way of achieving coverage. If a visual event is planned, it is wise to send a press release to the picture editors of the newspapers and the television news-desks, describing what will be taking place and why it is significant.

It is uneconomical to automatically send press releases out to everyone on the contact list. Press contacts can be put into various categories of interest. Word-processors make it simple to send out different versions of the same release to different audiences.

Once a press release is distributed, journalists may telephone for further details. These calls need to be dealt with promptly and thoroughly. This means having a 'press pack' ready to hand. This should supplement press releases with further information about the campaign and the organisation behind it. Handling press inquiries requires having someone properly briefed to answer press inquiries. Before dealing with the press it is worth thinking about the kinds of questions that may be asked, perhaps writing down a list of the ten hardest questions, to which effective answers can be prepared. It is also worth drawing up a list of 'quotable quotes' that summarise the key points and arguments underpinning the shareholder action.

In addition to press releases, it is sometimes worth holding a press conference. Press conferences should be used only when there is something particularly interesting to say, otherwise the press will not attend them. Typically, press conferences are held when people launch a campaign or publish a report, or have unearthed some startling new material. Generally speaking, press releases and contacts with journalists will be the most effective way of getting things into print. If a press conference is proposed, it should be short and well planned, beginning with a brief speech outlining the reason for the conference. It is common for larger campaigns to be 'launched' at a press conference. A launch lets the press know formally that there is a new campaign running. Invitations should be sent out as widely as possible, and should contain the same kind of information as a press release. A common practice is to invite a sympathetic public figure who is well known and respected to chair the launch.

Other Ways of Using the Press

More straightforward approaches to getting publicity in a newspaper include writing a letter to the editor of a newspaper. These have to be very short and so can only contain one or two points. They also have respond to something that has appeared recently in the newspaper. Another way of gaining press coverage is to take out an advertisement in a newspaper. This can be very expensive. A full-page advertisement in a national newspaper costs many thousands of pounds. A small advert on the financial pages asking for support from shareholders and others may be worthwhile. Alternatively, there are many other smaller-circulation newspapers, whose advertising rates are cheaper, in which an advert might prove more valuable. Examples are religious newspapers such as the *Church Times* or *The Friend*; magazines of pressure groups, such as Friends of the Earth's *Earth Matters*; 'issue' magazines like *Green Magazine* or *New Internationalist*; and specialist shareholder magazines like *Investors Chronicle*.

The above are general points about how to achieve coverage on shareholder action in the press.[54] While it is possible to get some coverage in the press by developing a good feature story about the issues and the company, generally speaking a press story needs to be a story about something — press releases have to inform the press about some *event* that has taken place, or is about to take place. There are a large number of activities available to shareholders which can be presented to the press as events worthy of coverage. Many of these activities will be useful for influencing targets on their own account (whether they are reported in the press or not). These are covered in the next chapter.

Organisational Issues

It is worth briefly considering the basic organisational structures that are necessary for achieving the professionalism, persistence and attention to detail that are prerequisites for successful shareholder action. The range of supporting work that needs to be done for shareholder action includes:

- Fund-raising.
- Financial administration.
- Adopting the appropriate legal/organisational structure.
- Producing publicity material.
- Dealing with the press.
- Maintaining the information/filing system.
- Answering press and public inquiries.
- Soliciting public support.
- Maintaining the membership.
- Coordinating coalitions with other groups.

Some of these issues are self-explanatory, some have already been alluded to, and others will be covered subsequently in the appropriate places. The rest are covered here.

Fund-raising and Membership

The process of taking shareholder action can be costly. Activities like putting resolutions to AGMs, preparing publicity leaflets, mailing out press releases, putting together presentation packs to lobby institutional investors, travelling to investors and company AGMs, doing research, buying shares, keeping in touch with supporters, and maintaining office equipment, all cost money. While raising money in the voluntary sector is not easy, there are a variety of possible sources. For shareholder action, the four primary sources are:

● Supporters/membership.

● Charitable trust funds.

● Activist charities.

● Institutional investors.

The idea of a membership supported organisation is an attractive one. Not only do members provide income (1,000 members paying a £15 annual fee produces a revenue of £15,000), but they also provide a source of practical support for activities like letter writing campaigns, press stunts, and attending AGMs. Some members may even be in a position to influence institutional investors — in the Fisons peat campaign, one local Friends of the Earth supporter turned out to be a trustee of a large public sector employees pension fund. However, while members are very useful, they carry a cost. Not only do they require considerable administrative work but, in order to keep members interested enough to renew their subscription, they need to be regularly kept in touch with the campaign's activities. Most groups respond to this need by producing a news sheet, often on a quarterly basis. For a membership of say 1,000, this can involve a considerable amount of time, and cost several hundreds of pounds to produce and distribute. The effective cost may be reduced by the fact that newsletters can be an useful way of keeping the press and the public informed, and of recruiting additional support.

Whether a group opts to invite membership or not, it is likely to need other sources of finance, particularly if it wishes to employ anyone or take any large scale action. The key sources of this funding are charitable trusts. There are around 1,500 large trusts in Britain that distribute over £10,000 annually in grants. The trusts have been set up largely by wealthy philanthropists over the last 100 years or so. Charitable trusts derive their income from the return on the investment of the capital supplied by their benefactors. The size of the capital held by these charitable trusts ranges from tens of thousands to tens of millions of pounds. Each year, the investment income on these sums, which the trustees are able to distribute, ranges from a few thousand pounds to a few million. Acquiring a share of this money is a very competitive process. Most trusts have specific policies which control the way the trustees distribute grants. These specify the kinds of activity in which the recipients must be engaged in order to qualify. The policies can also specify the geographical area, the religious orientation, and the status (charitable or otherwise) of successful applicants. Information about the trusts and their policies is provided by *A Guide to Major Trusts*, (1991 Edition), published by the Directory of Social Change, and the *Directory of Grant Making Trusts* published biennially by the Charities Aid Foundation. In addition, *Raising Money From Trusts* by Michael Norton gives detailed advice about how to go about trust fundraising (see appendix for details).

Currently, only a couple of dozen of the major trusts are likely to have any interest in supporting shareholder action groups. In order to have any chance of securing a grant, therefore shareholder activists need to target the trusts that are interested in their area of activity (e.g., equal opportunities, the environment, socially responsible business). They then need to develop a carefully crafted prospectus outlining, fairly briefly, the purpose of the project, a detailed plan for its implementation, the timescale, the budget, and some biographical details of the people involved in it. It is worth ensuring that the proposal is tailored as carefully as possible to the specific policies of the individual trusts concerned. When drafting a budget it is important to be realistic; trustees are unlikely to fund projects that are under-budgeted — so a budget that includes an annual wage bill of £5,000 for a full-time member of staff will not be looked upon favourably. It is worth ringing up the secretary of the trust to ask whether the trust has any special requirements.

There might, in certain cases, be some possibility that the larger campaigning groups or activist charities may consider supporting a shareholder action group if its objectives are sufficiently close to their objectives. Christian Aid, Friends of the Earth, Greenpeace, the World Development Movement, WWF and the Anti-Apartheid Movement have been involved in company action in the past. Another alternative source of finance is active institutional investors. As previously mentioned, in the USA over the last few years a growing number of large institutional investors have become highly active shareholders. This process is beginning to be duplicated in Britain, so there is a growing opportunity to attract institutional support for shareholder action. However, both charities and institutional investors are probably more likely to lend support within the framework of shareholder action coalitions, rather than by donating funds directly to a shareholder action group.

Coalitions

The most successful shareholder actions in Britain and the USA have been undertaken by coalitions of individuals and groups. Generally, the coalitions have tended to be divided into two kinds: coalitions of campaigning groups and coalitions of investor groups. There have been few full coalitions between campaigning groups and investor groups. This is partly because of the differences in motivation between the two kinds of groups: campaigning groups are mainly interested in changing corporate social policy and have little explicit interest in the financial performance of companies; investor groups are interested in financial performance, while seeing social responsibility as an important subsidiary issue. This basic difference tends to be reinforced by contrasts in culture and political outlook. To oversimplify the differences somewhat, investor groups are dominated by the trustees and fund managers of large institutions like pension funds and church investment funds, the careers of whom have been spent close to the financial establishment; campaigning groups, on the other hand, are run by socially motivated campaigners whose careers have been within more radical voluntary sector pressure groups. The consequence has been that many investor groups have been reluctant to become to closely involved with what they perceive to be extremist activist groups, and many campaigning groups have been deeply suspicious of being 'co-opted' by capitalist financial institutions. This is a caricature of the situation, and so not quite true — for example, many public sector pension fund trustees are trades unionists, and some pressure groups are socially conservative — nevertheless it is an instructive description.

In recent years, the two groups have been converging. The institutions are beginning to accept the importance of corporate social responsibility as well as financial performance, and are increasingly recognising their role in promoting it. Campaigning groups are learning to live with the financial community, and to develop 'market-friendly' campaigning strategies. However, there are still considerable disagreements between the two groups.

It is worth mentioning that disagreements are not simply between institutional investors and campaigners, there are large differences within these groups. In the campaigning sector there is a considerable amount of 'politics' between the numerous campaigning groups. In the investor sector there is often competition for business. Each campaigning group has its own institutional priorities and its own political position. Campaigning groups are also, to a certain extent, competing for the same media attention, for the same supporters, and for the same sources of finance. Fund managers and institutional investors are in a similar position, having to pander to various interest groups, or competing for customers. These considerations create serious problems for coalitions. In order to work, shareholder action needs well organised and well planned activity to take place over a period of years, with an explicit strategy and a clear set of objectives. In coalitions it is hard to achieve the level of coordination and commitment that is necessary, and it is especially hard to achieve the detailed agreement about strategy and objectives that is required. Many coalitions fail because these essential issues are fudged, so the coalition does not know precisely what it is trying to achieve.

Nevertheless, coalitions still provide good opportunities for effective shareholder action. So, rather than avoiding them, it is worth developing strategies for managing coalitions and making them work more effectively. Perhaps the most important objective is to build a structure and set of objectives for the coalition which all parties explicitly endorse and to which they are committed. The successful 1984 CLEAR campaign for unleaded petrol was run by a large coalition of groups. In order to ensure that it functioned properly the coalition members agreed to meet a number of requirements before joining. They had to contribute money and the time of one staff member; they had to send a representative to one of the campaign's main committees; they had to agree that their organisation would campaign on lead pollution issues in 1984; and they had to agree to contribute their knowledge and their experience of their field.[49] This is one sensible way of organising coalitions, but they can have other styles and structures. In some cases it is appropriate to have close knit coalitions with objectives agreed down to the minutiae of tactics, and with regular coalition meetings; in others it may be more appropriate for coalition members to keep arms-length relationships, agreeing to share information and broad objectives on a 'network' basis, but otherwise pursuing their own individual activities. Deciding what level of structure would be most appropriate to a particular coalition involves trying to understand the 'political' positions that exist within the coalition. This means trying to work out the individual interests and objectives of potential coalition partners, and imagining various ways of finding compromises on these interests. It is often useful, therefore, to see the prospective coalition partners as targets who need to be persuaded to participate, to adopt the most suitable form of coalition and the most appropriate strategy and objectives. While coalition partners are all on the same side, because they have their own particular interests and attitudes, they need to be persuaded in the same way as other targets of shareholder action.

Chapter 7
Taking Shareholder Action: Letters and Meetings

Letters to Companies

Individuals taking action on their own may lack the time or the inclination to involve themselves in the full range of campaigning action outlined in this book, but there remain other important forms of action that individuals may effectively pursue. The most obvious is writing letters to companies. Letters are also often the opening move in more substantial shareholder action campaigns. Letters to companies have many purposes. They provide an opportunity to seek information, to gauge the companies attitude, to set out a campaigning position, and to open up the way for dialogue. They also provide support for those within companies who are pushing for the same policy changes shareholder activists are pursuing, and provide management with a fair opportunity to respond to criticism before public action is taken.

Letters should be as specific as possible. If information is required from the company, the precise information must be asked for. Questions should be as unambiguous as possible, perhaps by phrasing the questions in such a way as to require a definite yes, no, or some quantitive data for their answer. This limits the ability of company word-smiths to evade the question by answering it with vague, pleasant platitudes, or answering a different question of their choice instead. The number of points, or requests, that each individual letter can effectively deal with is small. A letter making too many points is not only arduous for the people who have to answer it, but also allows them to respond to the points the company finds easy to deal with, and simply ignore the ones it finds difficult. Generally speaking, letters will have more chance of a reasoned response if they are phrased objectively, without too much emotion or opinion. In certain circumstances there may be a case for expressing concern more forcefully if it will be useful to bring home to the company the strength of feeling. If representatives of the company appear to be lying it is unwise to accuse them or risk libelling them in any way. Instead it may be better to present a factual case against their erroneous claim, or to tell them what the correct facts seem to be, asking the company to confirm them.

Letters, in the first instance, should probably be sent to the chief executive or the chairman by name (the names can be found in the annual report), although the reply to letters is usually handled by the public relations department. It is not necessary to be apologetic or diffident in the tone of the letter. Shareholders have a financial stake in the company, and in writing they are expressing their legitimate concern. Consequently, shareholders should expect a prompt, reasoned and comprehensive reply to their letters. If the company does not respond within a week or two, they should be pursued with a telephone call to the office of the person to whom the letter was sent, seeking confirmation that they have received it and asking when a response can be expected. Another letter may need to be sent, as companies regularly lose things, particularly if they have to pass them between departments. It may be worth faxing a second copy, to reinforce the urgency of the matter. If the shareholder action group represents a reasonably sized shareholding, it is important to make this clear to the company. If on the other hand it only owns a few shares, it is probably not worth mentioning the fact. Copies of all letters to the company and all the company's replies should be carefully filed. Perhaps one of the most important consequences of writing a letter to a company is that, generally speaking, companies will produce a written reply. This is valuable because anything that the company commits to paper is documentary evidence that can be used in future action, in a way that unrecorded spoken commitments cannot. A file of company correspondence is useful for information, but can also have other uses. For example, Father Patrick O'Mahoney, while a Catholic priest in Birmingham, wrote to 100 companies on behalf of his diocese. Some companies responded positively, others did not pay much attention to their replies. Subsequently Father O'Mahoney published his correspondence with the companies, to the embarrassment of those companies who failed to respond adequately.

Finally, it is worth emphasising that a company's reply to a letter should not be the end of an action, but the beginning of further action — a prompt for further questions and debate. Letters should usually be followed up, with thanks, a repeat of unsatisfactorily answered questions, and supplementary questions and points.

Orchestrated and Open Letters

Joint letters with pressure groups, institutional investors, or influential individuals can be more forceful than letters from individual shareholders. Depending on their purpose, these letters can either be sent confidentially or they can be published. In order to gain the signatures of influential groups and individuals, orchestrated letters of this kind have to be carefully presented. In order to get a range of support, it may be necessary to negotiate the content to the satisfaction of the signatories. Currently, few institutional investors in Britain will want to participate in such letters, particularly if they are made public, but this is changing, and it is likely that more will be prepared to do so in the future. While letters signed by institutional investors will be effective if they are sent privately, letters that are signed by influential individuals like MPs, journalists, authors, senior church people, academics and celebrities, tend to derive their effectiveness from publication, or the threat of publication. Open letters of this kind can be sent to the company accompanied by the warning of imminent publication, in the hope of winning concessions from the company to prevent this. Alternatively they can be distributed to the press straightaway. One way to guarantee coverage for an open letter is by paying for advertising space for it, but this is costly. A quarter-page advert in a broadsheet newspaper currently costs about £5,000.

Letter Writing Campaigns

Shareholder activists can also influence companies by persuading large numbers of the general public to write to a company about a specific issue. This works on the same basis as Amnesty International's letter writing campaigns. If a company receives a large number of letters about a specific issue it will tend to take a serious interest in the matter, on the principle that if 500 people are concerned enough to write to a company, there are probably tens of thousands of people worried about the issue. For letter writing campaigns to be useful, people need to be briefed about what to write and how to write it — letters should be polite, and factual rather than abusive tirades.

In 1992 Greenpeace organised a letter writing campaign to try to persuade ICI to stop its production of ozone destroying chemicals immediately. Greenpeace appealed to two different constituencies for the campaign: the general public, and doctors. Members of the public were asked to write, or send a pre-prepared postcard, to ICI's chief executive officer asking ICI to stop producing CFCs, and telling him that they would boycott ICI's Dulux paint 'until ICI stop destroying the ozone layer'. Doctors were approached for two reasons. Firstly because they have to deal with the cancers arising from ozone depletion, and secondly because ICI is a large manufacturer of prescription drugs. Greenpeace asked the doctors, where possible, to stop prescribing ICI drugs (or the drugs made by Stuart, its subsidiary) and prescribe alternatives instead, to put campaign literature in their surgeries, and to write to ICI voicing their concern. According to Greenpeace, over 4,000 family doctors participated in the campaign. ICI is reportedly speeding up their planned phasing out of CFC production.

Another technique Amnesty use to enhance the impact of their letter writing campaigns is the 'Urgent Action' letter. The aim of Urgent Action is to respond very swiftly to new developments. So, for example, if a company wins a bid for a project to build a dam, a shareholder activist version of the Urgent Action programme would aim to ensure that over the following few days the company receives 100 letters, faxes and telegrams, from around the world, expressing concern about the environmental impact of the dam. Above all, Urgent Actions require excellent organisation. The very speed of response can have a powerful effect on the company's perception of the public interest in its activities. It gives the company a very clear sense that its every move is being watched.

Meetings with Companies

Companies often invite individuals and groups with whom they have had correspondence to meet with them. These meetings are usually handled by representatives from companies' public relations departments. Meetings can be valuable because they open up more genuine dialogue and they allow a fuller exchange of views. Because meetings are informal and face-to-face, and are sometimes off-the-record, company representatives tend to be rather more candid than they are prepared to be in written communication. This gives shareholder activists a much better opportunity to evaluate the real chances of change in the company, to get a clearer idea of the real targets for action, and to establish the best route to the campaign's objectives. Meetings offer companies an opportunity to change their position before shareholder action moves to more public campaigning activity. Meetings can also contribute to shareholder activists' credibility both within the company and with journalists, shareholders and others outside the company. They strengthen the company's perceptions of the shareholders' concerns, and can give management the impression that they are dealing with reasonable people who are prepared to debate and enter into dialogue. Furthermore, the fact that shareholder activists are holding a meeting with the company on a particular issue may give decisive support for those in the company pressing for a policy change on that issue.

Finally, meetings offer opportunities for negotiation. If a shareholder campaign aims to take public action by, say, putting a resolution to the company's annual general meeting, then it is in quite a good position to prise concessions out of the company. The directors and public relations departments of large companies resent dissident resolutions and other public embarrassments caused by shareholder activists, particularly if they occur without any attempt at discussion or negotiation. Companies spend a considerable amount of money on generating positive images of themselves to the public. A well presented shareholder action can undo a significant amount of this work, giving the company a powerful incentive to prevent the action occurring. Often the easiest way for companies to prevent embarrassing action is for them to meet the activist group to see if there is anything that the company can offer to prevent the action from taking place. In the USA the pre-emptive negotiation of resolutions is perhaps the most effective single form of shareholder action. Around one-third of the oppositional resolutions proposed in the USA are withdrawn in return for concessions by the company. In 1986, the New York state pension fund, with investments of $54.4 billion, filed resolutions on divestment in South Africa with 121 companies in which it held investments. This led to negotiations with 70 of the 121 companies. Fifty-five of these companies agreed to withdraw their operations from South

Africa before the resolution went to the vote.[55] If the policy change the shareholder activists are trying to achieve is reasonable, and there are not decisive reasons for rejecting it, the threat to public relations of a dissident resolution may be all that is needed to tip the balance.

Preparation for Meetings

When meeting with companies there are at least three broad considerations:

1. Targets — with whom should the meeting occur?

2. Objectives — what needs to be discussed? What achievements can be hoped for?

3. Presentation — How should the meeting be conducted? How should the shareholder case be presented?

With whom the meeting should be held depends on what the objectives are. It may well be appropriate to discuss the issues at stake and the company's general position with junior representatives from the public relations department, but it is probably not appropriate to negotiate about withdrawing a resolution with such a representative. Shareholders have the right and responsibility to give their evaluations of company practices and to suggest alternatives to the highest rank of company officials. It is perfectly reasonable to request that the meeting be attended by someone of significant standing in the company — the head of public relations or one of the directors, for example.

During a face-to-face meeting with a representative of a company, it is even more important than usual to have a clear idea of objectives. When writing a letter there is plenty of time to think clearly about what has to be said and how it should be presented. At a meeting, on the other hand, there is no time to think things out properly, situations must be responded to as they arise. Thinking must therefore be done in advance. It is worth trying to prepare a position on each possible topic of discussion; working out what is the best that can be hoped for, what is the worst, and an acceptable compromise position. It is also worth trying to anticipate the sticking-points that might arise, and plan solutions to them. One way of limiting uncertainty is agreeing an agenda for the meeting with the company, although there is no guarantee it will be adhered to by the company. The agenda should not be too long: it is better to discuss a few issues properly rather than trying to raise everything that could possibly be discussed.

There are several things to be considered when deciding how to present a case at the meeting, from the basic question of which arguments and data to use to support the shareholder case, to more intangible questions about what could be called the 'interpersonal dynamics' of the meeting. Thinking about interpersonal dynamics involves shareholder activists in trying to imagine the motivations, pressures and outlook of the company representatives who will be attending the meeting, as well as thinking about their own feelings about the company, about their objectives, and about the people they will be encountering. Often, those involved in action on companies find themselves developing a hostile attitude to the company and its representatives. This is quite understandable when the company is particularly intransigent or unreasonable. It is not, however, helpful to bring this hostility to a meeting. Meetings usually require considered and controlled responses. Feelings of animosity interfere with this. The Interfaith Center for Corporate Responsibility's *Shareholder Manual* says 'Dialogue will involve you in an exchange permeated by value judgements, economic assumptions, and world views potentially conflicting with one another . . . there is more than one way for people of good will to assess moral obligations and the social good.' This is an effective, tolerant position from which to circumvent a combative, adversarial attitude, and move instead towards cooperation and agreement. There are a number of books written in this area, for example *Getting to Yes* by Roger Fisher and William Ury.

Perhaps the most important thing for shareholder activists to do is to take time before the meeting to examine their own attitudes, and to put themselves in the position of the company representatives. One way to get a better feel for the motivations, pressures and outlook of the company representatives is by doing role-plays of the meeting.

In order to develop a more positive attitude to the company, shareholders can try and see themselves as offering the company something positive. Church groups, for example can offer their ethical expertise, other groups may be able to offer specific advice on environmental issues, or on encouraging ethnic minority members to apply for jobs. Many groups will at least be able to offer the company a public relations advantage.

When meeting with the company, shareholders should have their arguments well rehearsed, with all the relevant background facts either memorized, or on a sheet of paper in front of them, so they can produce them when required. Shareholders should be able, if asked, to substantiate all the factual information they use by quoting its source, otherwise the company may find it easy to dismiss. This implies that shareholders should primarily use data from sources that *both* sides can reasonably accept as reliable. Shareholders can strengthen their case by demonstrating personal involvement in the issues, if possible, and using first-hand experiences to illustrate arguments. It may pay to invite 'experts' or influential figures to participate at the meeting. This can provide weight to the shareholder case, and can prevent too easy a brush-off by the company. It can, however, mean losing control of the discussion. Inviting 'outsiders' also requires agreement from the company.

Corporate Trickery

There is always a need for shareholders to be on their guard when dealing with companies. The public relations professionals that activists are dealing with are paid to be good at handling threats to the company's image. This sometimes requires ruthlessness. There are a number of ways that PR people can try and use the fact that shareholder activists have met the company to undermine their position. At the very least, if activists try and raise issues in public, say at the AGM, the company may try to dismiss their questions with the retort that 'the company has already gone to considerable lengths to answer your question on a previous occasion; the directors will be happy to talk with you further *after* the meeting' (i.e. out of the glare of publicity). There are, however, plenty of other ways for company chairmen to 'stonewall' questions at an AGM, so the fact that shareholders have had a meeting will probably not help the company too much. Nevertheless, campaigners should be careful what they say at meetings, and particularly what they agree to. Shareholders should avoid making questionable claims that can be proved wrong and repeated by the company in public to shareholders' discredit. They should avoid committing themselves to any substantial agreement, unless they are quite certain it is what they want to do — it is always possible to ask for time to consider it. Shareholders should be wary if the company offers to pay their expenses, or to take them out for a meal. The latter may be agreeable, and it provides an opportunity to get to know company contacts in an informal environment, which can lead to a more 'relaxed' discussion, but it is worth considering how such wining-and-dining might look to potential supporters.

Another thing shareholders should watch out for is that the company can quite easily turn a meeting into a public relations event. This can be mutually valuable, but it can make the campaigners' relationship with the company look too cosy. If shareholder activists do not want any publicity for their meeting, they should agree with the company that the meeting will be off-the-record, and that the press will not be contacted about it. This is binding on the activists as well, which might be disadvantageous: not being able to report publicly what occurred at the meeting can make it hard to verify that what the company says is true. It can also be hard to hold them to what they say, or even to get them to admit that they said what they said. If activists later try and make public what the company told them privately, not only will they look bad for breaking a confidentiality agreement, the company will also be able to deny all knowledge of it. Ideally, a happy medium should be agreed, where both sides can speak frankly in private, but that any substantive claims or commitments can be made public. One way of being clear about this is to submit to the company a draft of the parts of the discussion that are allowed to be made public, asking whether the company think it is a fair summary of the main points, and informing them of the possibility that the material will be made public. In order to do this, shareholders will need to take detailed notes of the meeting, which is a good idea in any case. To do this it is worth taking someone along to the meeting specifically to take notes. Lest this section gives a too sinister picture of companies, it should be noted that most companies will behave honourably and will not sink to subterfuge, particularly if activists behave decently with them. But it is not worth banking on it.

Chapter 8
Taking Shareholder Action: Formal Action at Company AGMs

Shareholder Resolutions

The most significant arena for shareholder action is the company's annual general meeting. Annual general meetings are the natural environment for shareholder action. When the company was invented as a legal institution in the 1850s, the general meeting of shareholders was considered the sovereign body of corporate democracy. In practice this is no longer very true. AGMs largely fail to provide a forum for shareholders to control companies by holding open debates about the details of their company's activities, and by holding the directors properly accountable. But while AGMs may not adequately fulfil their legally appointed role, they remain excellent opportunities for shareholder action. This is because they are public occasions, attended by all the main targets that shareholder activists need to influence: the company directors, the company's public relations team, many of the big institutional investors, the more active small-shareholders, and the financial press. AGMs offer good opportunities to publicise and dramatise issues to the target groups of shareholder action. More importantly, AGMs offer a unique opportunity for shareholders activists because they are the crucial annual public relations events for companies. Consequently, at AGMs companies are more vulnerable than usual, providing shareholder activists with unusually strong leverage.

Legally, annual general meetings are considered to be the ultimate source of authority in companies. They are the one place where shareholders can, in theory, exercise real control. This is reflected by the fact that the law gives the shareholders voting at AGMs wide-ranging powers. The shareholders may, by simple majority, pass resolutions to appoint or dismiss directors, to appoint or dismiss the company's auditors, to adopt or reject the company's annual report and accounts, and they may, in many companies, dictate general corporate policy. Furthermore, AGMs are compulsory: whether the directors like it or not they must call an AGM each calender year, and not more than 15 months after the last one. This means that AGMs offer the legal potential for shareholders to exert their control over the company.

In practice, however, these opportunities are rarely exploited. The legal framework no longer operates as it was meant to. The law is framed in the expectation that the shareholders will want to wield their power at meetings, that they will want to scrutinise the directors' activities. In reality, in large British companies, this expectation is not supported by the facts. Shareholders are unwilling or unable to hold directors properly accountable. Instead the relationship is reversed: the directors have pretty much absolute authority over the shareholders. This is partly because the law, as it stands today, is stacked so much in the directors' favour. Consequently it is only in the most extraordinary circumstances that shareholders are able to get a resolution passed against the opposition of the directors. As a result, few resolutions opposing the directors are put to meetings, and even when they are they attract only a few percent of the votes. One set of reasons for this places the blame with the shareholders themselves. Normally British shareholders are apathetic about becoming actively involved with their company. Usually only a tiny fraction of shareholders, less than 1%, attend meetings. Even when something dramatic happens and the shareholders react, the common shareholder response is to follow the advice of the directors, rather than taking an independent position. Consequently a shareholder canvassing backing for an oppositional resolution is unlikely to get much support. This problem is compounded by the fact that in large companies today there are often hundreds of thousands of shareholders; contacting them all about a resolution is a difficult and hugely expensive process; prohibitively so for most shareholders. Fortunately the Companies Act has provision for shareholders making resolutions to have access to the company's own mechanisms for contacting its members, but even using this has its problems, as we shall see.

Another set of difficulties faced by shareholders putting oppositional resolutions is in the conduct of the meeting itself. It is the directors, not the shareholders, who set the agenda of the shareholders' meeting, and it is usually the chairman of the board of directors, rather than a shareholder, who chairs the meeting. This means that the directors bring considerable influence to bear on the process of debating and voting on resolutions, effectively controlling the process of the meeting.

A further obstacle for the success of oppositional resolutions is the proxy voting system. Together with the formal notice of the annual general meeting, individual shareholders also receive a proxy voting form. The proxy form provides opportunity for those shareholders not attending the meeting, usually the vast majority, to appoint a proxy to vote in their place. The proxy form also contains a list of the resolutions to be voted on at the meeting, with space for shareholders to mark their preference for or against the resolution. It is standard practice for the vast majority of shareholders who bother to return their forms, to nominate the chairman of the board of directors as their proxy. This means that even before the meeting takes place, the directors have a majority of the shareholders' votes in their pocket. So, irrespective of any discussion taking place at the meeting, most shareholders' votes are already committed to supporting the management position, making the voting that takes place in the meeting a mere formality.

These problems make it quite unrealistic to imagine that oppositional shareholders can simply present a good and persuasive case to a shareholders' meeting, and thereby secure a majority vote for a change in company policy. Even in America where oppositional shareholder action is common, oppositional resolutions rarely get more than a small percentage the vote at meetings. Fortunately, getting majority-votes is not the only possible aim for putting resolutions. A resolution that gets even a couple of percent of the vote can have large publicity potential. It is this that makes resolutions useful for shareholder action. Not only do they allow shareholders to raise issues in a very public and concrete manner but, more importantly, resolutions, or at least the threat of bringing them to an AGM, can provide a powerful lever for influencing the corporate policy process.

Annual general meetings are formal, public events, attended by all the main targets of shareholder action. Consequently, making a powerful argument at an AGM saves shareholder activists from having to make the same argument separately to all their individual targets audiences. AGMs are also useful for extracting information about the company from the directors and getting them to make public, on-the-record statements about policy. AGMs are 'privileged' occasions where usual standards for libel are suspended, which offers opportunities for a frank exchange of opinions. They also provide a valuable annual focus for a wider campaign on an issue or a company.

As already stated, AGMs are attended by most of the targets shareholder activists want to influence. Many members of this target group of individuals and institutions are also vitally important for the company. This group contains the people upon whose opinions financial confidence in the company rests. In order to raise investment capital, companies require the confidence of the financial markets. Confidence in a company depends to a large extent on the opinions of institutional shareholders, fund managers, creditor banks, City analysts and influential financial journalists. That is to say, just the kind of people who watch what happens at AGMs. Consequently the directors try to make sure that AGMs are slickly managed public relations events. Shareholder activists, on the other hand, have a unique opportunity to get their voices heard publicly by all the right people. This is uncomfortable for companies, and many will be prepared to make concessions in order to avoid the potential embarrassment of noisy opposition at the AGM.

The primary opportunities for shareholder activists to influence company policy depend on the use of formal and informal tactics to put *pressure* on company management; rather than the attempt by shareholder activists to secure majority votes on resolutions. While the formal, legal tools of shareholder control do not do the job they were designed for, they should not be discarded. A resolution proposed by oppositional shareholders will almost never secure a majority vote, but it may be an excellent way of attracting further attention to the issue and building support for it. In addition, informal opportunities at AGMs, like distributing campaign leaflets to other shareholders, while having no place in the law, can have a useful role in furthering campaign objectives. The rest of this section describes the legal requirements that have to be met for using the formal tools available to shareholders.

Putting Resolutions

There are four kinds of formal, shareholder tools available: putting resolutions to the AGM, proposing amendments from the floor, voting on resolutions, and asking questions of directors. Of the four the first is the most significant but the hardest to use. Resolutions cannot simply be presented for discussion and a vote by a shareholder from the floor of the AGM. Instead, resolutions must be submitted well in advance, and must jump several hurdles before they can even be added to the AGM agenda.

Resolutions are simply written proposals that are voted on by the shareholders. They are the primary legal vehicle by which shareholders are supposed to be able to exert their ultimate rights of control on the company. They can be used to change the composition of the board of directors, to change the basic structure of the company, and in many companies, to change corporate policy. But in practice they tend not to be used for these purposes. Instead the vast majority of resolutions currently brought before British company meetings are those specifically required by the law. These routine resolutions are for the annual re-appointment of the auditors, the re-election of directors, the adoption of the annual directors report and accounts. These resolutions are usually brought before the meeting in the name of the board of directors, rather than by independent shareholders. They are almost invariably passed on a show of hands by the shareholders at the meeting, after little or no discussion.

There are three different types of resolutions: special, extraordinary and ordinary. In order to be passed, the first two require at least a three-quarters majority vote at a general meeting, while ordinary resolutions only need a straight majority. The first two kinds of resolutions apply to certain special types of business, such as changing a company's articles of association. The ordinary resolutions are for more normal activities, and are the ones of most concern here. In Britain, there are few resolutions currently brought before AGMs by shareholders who are independent of the board. Many large British companies go for years without having to face an oppositional resolution at the AGM. However, in Britain in the last decade and a half there have been a number of resolutions on social issues, for example in 1977 at the Midland Bank PLC AGM on loans to South Africa, in 1984 at the Shell AGM concerning its supply of oil to South Africa, and to B.A.T

Industries PLC) demanding information about its tobacco marketing policy. In 1992 a resolution was brought before Wellcome PLC in an attempt to cut shareholders dividends in order to invest more in Aids research. All these resolutions were easily beaten, for example the Shell result was 84 million votes against to 4 million votes for. The 4 million positive votes came from a number of sympathetic institutional investors like local authority pension funds, union funds, and the late Greater London Council. As we have seen in previous sections of this book, the situation is radically different in America, where hundreds of oppositional resolutions on social issues are made annually.

The reason that resolutions have been little used in Britain for getting companies to change their policies is partly because resolutions require a lot of work and organisation, and partly because it is assumed that as dissident resolutions are unlikely to get more than a small proportion of the vote they are not worthwhile. The first reason is valid, but the second is not, as it ignores the other purposes to which resolutions can be put.

Getting a Resolution onto the AGM Agenda

The steps required by the law for bringing an ordinary resolution before an AGM are as follows:

1. *Lodging a resolution*: resolutions must be put in writing and deposited at a registered office of the company. The company must receive the resolution at least 28 days before the date of the meeting, or at anytime before the meeting is formally announced by the company.[56] In a few special cases (e.g. a resolution for the dismissal of a director), more time must be allowed.

2. *Circulating a resolution*: For a resolution to be dealt with at the AGM, it is not enough that the company has a copy of it on time. It must also be circulated to the shareholders. This circulation must take place, as far as is practicable, at the same time and in the same manner as the notice of the meeting. This usually means that it should be distributed with the 'proxy forms' circulated to all voting shareholders before the AGM.

3. *Requiring directors to circulate a resolution*: While a resolution must be circulated to the shareholders before it may appear on the AGM agenda, the directors do not have a duty to circulate a resolution they receive unless it meets certain demanding conditions. If it fails to meet these conditions, then, unless shareholders undertake to circulate it themselves (a practically impossible task), the resolution cannot appear on the agenda. The conditions for requiring the directors to circulate a resolution are:

a. A 'requisition' asking for circulation of the resolution must be received by the company at least six weeks prior to the meeting, or any time before notice of the meeting is given to shareholders.

b. It must be signed by either shareholders with at least 5% of the voting rights of the company, or alternatively at least 100 shareholders, who have paid an average of at least £100 each for their shares.

c. The requisition must be accompanied by enough money to meet the cost to the company of circulating the resolution to the other shareholders.

Once these requirements are met, the directors then are required by law to circulate notice of the resolution. The law also requires them to distribute a statement of up to 1,000 words, supplied by the requisitioning shareholders, explaining their resolution. However, even if all these onerous requirements are met, there are still further potential difficulties. It is possible for those objecting to the resolution to apply to the courts to prevent the resolution from being circulated. If this approach is to be successful, the objectors must prove that the resolution is attempting to 'secure needless publicity of a defamatory manner'.[57] In practice this provision does not seem to be used often, and for most resolutions could not be used. Of more concern are the practical problems that may be confronted in meeting the standard legal requirements outlined above. They can be divided into three kinds — numbers, timing, and expense.

Meeting the Shareholder Numbers Requirement for Resolutions

There are two options for meeting the shareholding-size condition (3.b, above) which has to be achieved before the company is required to circulate a resolution. The first involves getting support from the owners of 5% of the voting shares in the company. In a big company, 5% ownership requires an investment running to tens or hundreds of millions of pounds, so unless several very big institutional shareholders can be persuaded to sign the requisition, the second option is the only viable one. This condition requires the signatures of 100 shareholders. These shareholders must have paid an *average* of £100. So if two shareholders, who paid £5,000 each for their shares, sign up, then the other 98 signatories need only own a single share each. Note that the condition requires an average of £100 to have been *paid* for the shares, not their present market value. There are a number of ways of building this hundred. If the individual or group proposing the resolution has £10,000 available for a, perhaps risky, medium term investment, it is then quite straightforward to get together 100 people who are prepared to be shareholders, if only in name, and buy the necessary shares.

If this is not possible or desirable, signatures will have to be solicited from other existing shareholders. Complete lists of company shareholders are obtainable from Companies House.[58] Companies House has registers of the names and addresses of the shareholders of all British limited companies. These lists can be viewed either by visiting Companies House offices in Cardiff or London, or by buying microfiche versions of the lists by post. Access to this service from Companies House only costs a few pounds. However, for large companies with tens of thousands of shareholders the list will be very long, most of the shareholders will be unknown, and many shareholdings will be held in the name of nominee financial institutions, like banks. So unless one is looking for specific names, or seeking to do a mail-shot to a random sample of shareholders, such a list is of limited value.

An alternative strategy is to approach organisations that have already been involved with shareholder action. These organisations may have contacts amongst individual and institutional shareholders, who are prepared to participate in the proposing of resolutions. In addition to investor organisations, many ordinary pressure groups are interested in company action, and may be willing to provide contacts and support for resolutions. In addition to providing contact names, pressure groups might agree to publishing a short article in their members' news sheet, providing information on the resolution, and appealing for support from investors and other interested groups.

The Timing of
Resolution Submissions

The first problem in timing preparations for the resolution is that the actual date for the AGM is not announced until a few weeks before the meeting occurs. As the deadlines for filing resolutions are relative to this date, it is impossible to work out the deadline date until the announcement is made, by which time it may be too late. But, while the exact date is unknown, companies tend to hold their AGMs during the same couple of months each year, so an approximation is possible. The minimum notice period for lodging an ordinary resolution is 28 days before the AGM. However, in order for it to be circulated, the requisition for the circulation of the resolution must be in the company's hands at least six weeks before. So six weeks is the basic legal deadline for getting a resolution to a company. However, in practice, even six weeks may not be enough. The law requires directors to notify the shareholders of the resolution 'in the same manner and (so far as is practicable) at the same time as the notice of the meeting'.[59] This effectively means that the resolution should appear with all the other resolutions on the proxy form. Proxy forms, however, may be printed and sent to shareholders more than six weeks before the AGM. If this happens, and the resolution is submitted at the six week deadline, then the company will have to make a separate mailing for the dissident resolution. The company is then allowed to charge those proposing the resolution with costs for this, entailing very substantial extra expense. So the requisition needs to be with the company before the proxy forms are printed, perhaps as long as two to three months before the meeting. It is a good idea to try and find out from the company secretary, when precisely the proxy forms will be printed, so that the requisition can be sent in good time. But even with this precaution, it is always possible that an unhelpful company could change its mind, and publish the forms ahead of this date. The only reliable way to avoid frustration seems to be to give the requisition to the company as early as several months before the meeting. But giving too much time carries disadvantages. The more time the directors have a resolution in their possession, the more time they have to prepare a detailed case and solicit investors' support against it. This is probably not too important, because even the legal minimum of 28 days is time enough for a company to mobilise a team of lawyers and public relations advisors to develop a counter-attack.

The timeframe provided by these minimum requirements is only part of the time required for organising a resolution. If a dissident shareholder group is able to buy the necessary £10,000 worth of shares itself, then it needs only to ensure that it does so in good time to have all the 100 shareholders registered before they put their name to the requisition document. Alternatively, if the resolution is to be signed by one hundred existing shareholders, time needs to be allocated to get their support. It might take several months to contact, and perhaps meet with, the hundred or so shareholders needer to make the requisition. It would therefore be reasonable to start preparing a resolution six months or more before the AGM usually takes place.

The Cost of Proposing Shareholder Resolutions

The law requires (3.c, above) the requisitioning shareholders to pay the costs of the circulation of their resolution and accompanying statement. This can be expensive. If the requisition for the resolution is deposited with the company before the proxy forms are printed, then the costs of circulation should merely be those for a few sentences of extra print on the forms. But as many listed companies have over 100,000 shareholders, each requiring a proxy form, paying for the few extra lines of print could run to hundreds of pounds. And if the printing deadline for the proxy forms is missed the expense soars. In 1992 a group of shareholders tried to bring a resolution before the AGM of one of the newly privatised water companies. The shareholders complied with the legal requirements and put in their requisition. However they were told that the proxy forms had already been printed. The company informed them it would cost around £5,000 to circulate the extra forms containing the resolution and accompanying statement to all the shareholders as a separate mail-out. It is therefore vital to submit the requisition before the proxy form printing deadline.

One faint hope is offered by a provision in the law which allows the shareholders to vote at the AGM to get the company to bear the costs of circulating an oppositional resolution. But as dissident resolutions usually only receive a small fraction of AGM votes, it is unlikely that oppositional shareholders would be successful at achieving a majority vote for a refund. Another avenue that has been successfully pursued is to negotiate with the company to get it to agree to waive the charge of costs. A resolution that was brought before the Midland Bank AGM in 1977 was circulated at no charge as a gesture of goodwill on behalf of the company.

Another potential source of expense is the legal advice that may be necessary to guarantee that the wording of the resolution is tight and in the correct legal form. It is possible to bring resolutions to AGMs without legal advice, particularly if advice is taken from people who have experience of company procedures. However professional legal advice minimises the risk of any loose wording in the resolution. This prevents ambiguities which may allow the company to side-step or dismiss the resolution without having to debate it properly. Legal fees for consultation can be several hundred pounds. However there is a chance that a sympathetic lawyer may be persuaded to offer a concessionary rate, or give free advice. Alternatively one of the other signatories to the requisition may be persuaded to meet these costs. It is worth contacting PIRC, which has considerable experience with legal aspects of shareholder action, about whom to approach for legal advice.

One important caveat that applies to the whole of this chapter, is that while most of the legal principles discussed are minimum legal standards that all companies must adopt, some variety is allowed by the law. Individual company articles regularly specify different procedures for dealing with resolutions and other governance matters. This can work in the shareholder activists' favour, as is the case of companies which allow an individual shareholder to nominate directors; but differences often work to make the shareholder activists' job harder. It is worth buying a copy of the company's articles of association for a few pounds from Companies House, which details the company's special rules.

The Content of Resolutions

The above outlines the principle regulations for proposing resolutions at AGMs. But there are additional regulations covering the content of resolutions. Shareholders cannot simply resolve whatever they want. The most significant restrictions are those imposed by the articles of association of each particular company. The articles distribute the control of the company between the shareholders and the directors. Some kinds of control can only be exercised by the general meeting of shareholders, others can only be exercised by the directors. Some articles rule that the shareholders may not instruct the directors on matters of general policy, others give a relatively free rein. The basic rule of thumb is that if the content of a resolution is not expressly prohibited by the articles, or by the law then the resolution will be acceptable. The kinds of resolution that are made by oppositional shareholders fall into several categories, including: requests for the directors to change policy, requests for the company to disclose information and resolutions for the appointment or dismissal of directors. In the USA, resolutions for the disclosure of information have been particularly successful. Information resolutions (for example, one requesting the company to prepare a report on the numbers of ethnic minority members it employs at various levels) serve to increase accountability and as a platform for future action. They also tend to be rather less controversial than other kinds resolutions.

Perhaps the most important kind of resolution in many companies are those to appoint and dismiss directors. If shareholders can decide the shape of the board of directors, they can effectively control the policy and decision making of the company. But it is overwhelmingly the case in Britain that the resolutions to appoint directors are proposed by the directors, not the shareholders, and that these resolutions are almost always passed, making the board of directors a self-perpetuating oligarchy rather than the agents of the shareholders. However, some attempts have been made by shareholder activists to propose their own directors. In fact one of the very first 'social' shareholder resolutions in the USA, in 1970, was a motion to General Motors (GM) proposing

> 'That management expand the board to allow representation of constituencies heretofore ignored by the company: women, blacks, consumers, and environmentalists.[60]

The resolution was not passed by the shareholders, but the motion caused extensive debate in the AGM and elsewhere. In response GM appointed the Reverend Leon Sullivan to the board. Rev. Sullivan was the first African-American to sit on the board of a major US company. He described his role at the company as 'a voice from the outside on the inside'.[61] Sullivan later gave his name to a code of good practice relating to the operation of US companies in South Africa.

Rather than asking a company to expand the board, the shareholders can propose a resolution to dismiss a director and appoint someone in his or her place.[62] Special notice must be given of these resolutions, and the director concerned has the right of reply which must be sent to all members accompanying the resolution for his or her dismissal. The law states that no single resolution can be made to appoint more than two directors at once. Directors cannot be appointed if they are over 70 years old.

Resolutions should be phrased as clearly and unambiguously as possible. As the point of submitting a resolution is rarely to attempt to get a majority vote, resolutions need not aim to be legally watertight; this is essential only for shareholders who expect to get a resolution passed. If that is the aim, then the resolution must be drafted with its practical implementation in mind. This generally means it must be so carefully worded that there is no way that the directors can avoid implementing it. If, on the other hand, the point of the resolution is to gain publicity or to put pressure on the directors, such a resolution is not necessarily the most appropriate. A legally watertight resolution usually requires extensive and incomprehensible legal jargon, with numerous clauses covering all possible eventualities. This renders such a resolution impenetrable to the other shareholders or the press and this makes it hard to use a publicity tool. The alternative is to draft the resolution clearly and simply, so its principles are immediately obvious. After all, it is unlikely to be passed without the directors' support, but if it is clearly written might serve to raise important issues for debate.

Companies are generally hostile to shareholder resolutions. At the moment in Britain, dissenting resolutions are extremely rare, and so are considered by company officials as unduly aggressive forms of action. This need not be so. Shareholder resolutions are a proper part of the corporate governance process. They are after all, at one level, simply the legal expression of the shareholders' right, as members of the company, to have a say in its policy and management. Perseverance in educating company officials seems to pay off. Shareholder activists involved in the long term campaign to get Shell to divest itself of its South African operations, report a considerable shift over several years in the company's attitude to action. The debate on South Africa has become an almost institutionalised part of the AGM and the company's reporting process.

One way of soothing the company when presenting a resolution is for shareholder activists to keep it informed of their intentions. It is probably worth contacting the company secretary to discuss the formal procedure for putting the resolution to the meeting. It may also be worth sending a copy of the resolution to the company chairman, asking him to put it to the board meeting to see whether they may be interested in adopting it as policy, without it having to go to an AGM. It is very unlikely that the directors will adopt the resolution in this way, but it will focus their attention on the issue and opens up the space for a dialogue on the resolution.

As mentioned earlier, one of the more effective forms of shareholder action used in the USA is the negotiated withdrawal of resolutions. This is a bit like the practice of settling civil legal cases, like libel claims, 'out of court'. What happens is the shareholders' group gathers support for the resolution, goes through the motions of proposing it, while making it known that it is willing to be flexible. If the company decides that it would rather make a few concessions than risk bad publicity from a dissident resolution, it will offer to discuss the resolution. The shareholders' group then negotiates with the company. If it is able to get the company to agree to satisfactory concessions, it withdraws the resolution. While this is a tried and tested process in the USA, in Britain, since so few oppositional resolutions are proposed, this kind of negotiation has not happened to any great extent.

Voting on Resolutions at AGMs

Compared with the process of getting resolutions on to the agenda of an AGM, voting on them is easy. Most resolutions are simply put to the meeting by the chairman, with a few words of explanation, and, in the first instance at least, the outcome is decided by a show of hands. Either the chairman or the shareholders may, however, demand a ballot instead. On a show of hands the motions are decided on the basis of one person one vote, whereas on ballot they are decided on the basis of one share one vote. This difference derives from an old principle of equity amongst shareholders. That is to say that individual shareholders should have equal control, irrespective of the number of shares they own. This principle was unsuccessfully defended in the 19th century[63] by a bill attempting to give small shareholders proportionally more votes than larger ones. The principle remains in the practice of voting by a show of hands and in the ability of any shareholder to ask questions in a general meeting, irrespective of size shareholding. For example at the 1992 AGM of The RTZ Corporation PLC, seven oppositional shareholders, holding a handful of shares each, took up almost half of the two hour duration of the meeting.

The alternative to voting by a show of hands, one shareholder one vote, is to hold a poll, where voting is weighted according to size of shareholding. Polls involve shareholders putting their name, and the number of shares they own, on a ballot paper. All voting shareholders are entitled to demand a poll instead of, or in addition to, a vote. However they can only guarantee success in this demand if it is supported by at least five shareholders, including shareholders' proxies (Except if the company follows Table A of the 1985 Companies Act where only two members are required), or a shareholder with 10% of the total shareholdings. The chairman on the other hand can always demand a poll whenever he wants. Polls can be requested either after a vote by a show of hands has taken place, or instead of one. The poll, if successfully demanded, need not take place at the meeting, but at some time in the future, usually requiring another meeting, as postal ballots are not commonly allowed. According to Table A of the Companies Act 1985, if someone votes at a meeting but is not qualified to do so, they may be challenged and the chairman's decision is final. But only challenges made during the meeting in which the vote was cast are allowable.

Amendments to Resolutions

Amendments to resolutions can be made at the meeting so long as they fall within the scope of the notice of the resolution that was circulated to shareholders. Precisely what this means is open to some debate. Clearly if the notice for the resolution is vaguely worded then there is more scope for alteration than if it is very tightly worded. L.C.B.Gower, an influential company lawyer, has argued that amendments should reasonably be accepted to resolutions if they serve to reduce the burden of the resolution on the shareholders. The example Gower uses is if a resolution is proposed to increase the directors' salaries by £10,000, an amendment to lower the increase to £5,000 should be acceptable 'since a member who was prepared to swallow a camel could scarcely strain at a gnat'.[64] While this may be true for ordinary resolutions, arguments exist suggesting that, for special or extraordinary resolutions, amendments should not be accepted. The logic of limiting the scope for amendments is that shareholders should be able to decide whether they need to attend a meeting from the notice of the business of a meeting. If amendments that change the nature of the business at the meeting are accepted, then every shareholder would need to attend just in case an inoffensive resolution was changed into an offensive one by an amendment. While this is true, the logic seems at odds with the purpose of meetings. The point of shareholder's meetings is that shareholders meet to raise and debate issues before voting on resolutions. Allowing the amendment of resolutions could seem valuable to this process. Shareholders should not be merely rubber stamping issues that have been decided in advance prior to any debate. At present with the restrictive resolution process, this is precisely what happens. However, the law is not about to change, and amendments are currently not very common. But, as amendments, unlike resolutions, are easy to propose, it may be worth trying to move amendments to company resolutions. If the amendment changes the nature of the resolution it may be ruled out of order straight away, but if it only makes a small change it may be allowed. Thereby offering debating time to the proposer, and a vote. Alternatively, it is possible to use amendments to remove any problems arising with shareholder activists' own resolutions.

Shareholders' Proxies

In order to ensure that members who do not attend meetings can vote, the law makes provision for shareholders to appoint proxies to exercise their rights in their place. As only a tiny minority of shareholders attend AGMs, acting by proxy is a much used technique. Proxies are appointed by means of proxy forms. Proxy forms are commonly sent out to members with the notice of the AGM and with the annual report. These forms enable members appoint someone to be their proxy. They also enable members to register which way they wish their proxies to vote on the resolutions. For Stock Exchange listed companies proxy forms must be sent to all voting members with provision for two way voting on all resolutions to be put to the meeting.

For a proxy's appointment to be valid the company must be notified. This is quite straightforward as the proxy forms sent out to shareholders by the company are designed with this in mind. The Companies Act requires companies to accept notification of proxies up to a minimum of 48 hours before the meeting is due to take place, after this deadline companies do not have to accept new proxy nominations. Proxies may not vote on resolutions decided by a show of hands, but they may do so in a poll. This puts proxies at a disadvantage. However proxies have the right to demand a poll, and if they join with five other members or proxies their demand must be met.

In the past several companies have refused to allow shareholder activist proxies into the AGM, on the grounds that they have not received the proxy forms nominating the activists. This is a convenient excuse. It is therefore worth sending proxy forms by recorded delivery, leaving plenty of time before the deadline. Shell is one of several companies that have refused entry to proxies arranged by the End Loans to South Africa campaign (ELTSA). On one occasion when this happened, ELTSA had sent the proxy forms to the Shell company registrar by recorded delivery, and got Post Office confirmation that the forms had been received before the deadline. So when Shell claimed that they had not received the forms, ELTSA was able to prove that they had. Shell apologised for not letting the proxies in, and gave them a token payment for the inconvenience. This won coverage for ELTSA in *The Guardian*.

Legal doubt exists over whether proxies are required to vote in the way that the members who appointed them have requested on the proxy form. There is a strong argument that as the directors are entrusted with the proxy votes of members, they must follow their standard duty of trust. However this duty does not apply to proxies solicited by members, so in theory a proxy could vote in the opposite way to that specified by the appointing member. But there is probably some legal obligation for people who have solicited proxies to use them in the way that they have said they would. Of course if the proxy form is returned with no preferences either way the appointed proxy can use his or her discretion.

Soliciting Proxies

Usually members do not go out looking for people to be their proxy. It happens the other way round: proxies are solicited by the board of directors or, less commonly, by dissident shareholders. The proxy solicitation process is very unevenly balanced in favour of the board. Directors are *required* to explain their policy to shareholders and to appeal for their support, and they are allowed to use company money to pay for this. Dissident shareholders who wish to solicit proxies are in a much less favourable position. If they wish to use the company's soliciting mechanisms, they must go through the same complex process as shareholders wishing to force directors to circulate notice of resolutions before a meeting (see page 123). This can be difficult and expensive, so it may be more appropriate for dissident shareholders to approach proxies on a more informal basis. Merely finding out, via Companies House or elsewhere, who the other big shareholders are can be an expensive and time consuming task in itself. But a few dozen letters sent to carefully targeted institutions might be effective. Alternatively, shareholders can be solicited by advertising, either generally in the financial press, or specifically within the ethical investment movement.

There is obviously no special advantage to be gained in holding the proxy vote of someone who would otherwise attend the meeting and vote on the same side, but clearly there are advantages in trying to solicit the proxies of shareholders who will not attend the meeting. Shareholders who do not attend meetings are most likely to nominate the chairman as proxy, but some of them may be open to persuasion by carefully presented oppositional arguments. While it is desirable to obtain the proxies of these shareholders, there is more public relations potential to be gained by having them there to vote, to ask questions, and to speak to journalists in person. So if shareholders can be persuaded to deliver their proxy vote, it is worth trying to persuade them to go a step further and attend the meeting.

Asking Questions at AGMs

The law does not present detailed rules about asking questions at AGMs. The common practice is that the chairman asks for questions and selects questioners from the people who put up their hands. However there is no requirement for the chairman to allow time for everyone who wants to ask a question to do so, and chairmen regularly close meetings before all the questions have been answered. But if the chairman wishes to close the meeting, shareholders may demanded a vote to see whether it is the will of the meeting that he does so.[65] For oppositional groups who have created a positive impression at the meeting, it is possible that the chairman might be overruled by a poll of this kind. However, if the bulk of shareholders do not like what the oppositional shareholders are asking, or are hungry and want to go to lunch, then this tactic will not work. If the chairman closes a meeting and the oppositional shareholders are unhappy, if they own 10% of the voting capital of the company they can always requisition an extraordinary general meeting. But few oppositional shareholder groups have such a sizeable block of shares, making this alternative hypothetical. In practice therefore the chairman can usually close the meeting after allowing a reasonable number of questions lasting a reasonable length of time, whether there are still further questioners or not. A wise chairman ought to behave 'reasonably', partly because he risks alienating friendly shareholders if he seems unfair, and partly because it would not look good if he attempted to close a meeting just because shareholders were asking difficult questions.

It is up to the chairman to choose the questioners. Shareholders should consider how to maximise the chances of being selected. Shareholder groups that have a large number of people dispersed throughout the audience, dressed inconspicuously (i.e. smartly) to blend in, are probably most likely to be selected to ask questions. Shareholders who feel they have more questions to ask than the chairman will allow, can make noisy demands at the end of the meeting for the right to ask a question, with limited chances of success.

One alternative system that has been tried by some companies, is to ask shareholders to submit questions in advance of the AGM. These are then sorted into categories and an allegedly representative sample is taken. During the meeting, only those shareholders whose questions are deemed representative, are invited to put their questions. This is supposedly to ensure that the few questions that are allowed reflect the concerns of all the shareholders, and to allow the directors time to assemble the information that they need for full answers. But this method is not completely satisfactory. It is the directors who select the representative questions, it is therefore open to them to select only the comfortable questions, filtering out the ones they find awkward. This system also gives directors time to generate clever smoke-screen answers. One computer services company offers a computerised version of this procedure for AGMs. Shareholders are required to input their questions on a computer as they arrive at the meeting, the questions are sorted into categories, and despatched to company experts. These experts then draft up suitable answers which the chairman can read off the autocue that the computer company provides. The computer also filters out questions that can be adequately 'dealt with' outside the meeting by company officials. This is potentially even more unhelpful because it can serve to prevent shareholders from raising issues in front of the other shareholders, publicly. But, even after these written or computerised questions are asked and answered, it is still possible for shareholders to try and ask further questions, whether they have been submitted in advance or not. There is no reason why shareholders cannot simply put up their hands, or call for further questions from the floor of the meeting. If the chairman seeks to close the meeting in order to avoid answering these questions, then a vote may be demanded as before.

Annual general meetings are often held in big halls with poor acoustics. It is therefore usually necessary for the company to have a public address system, with a roving microphone for shareholders' questions. This gives the company even more control over the questions being asked. If the chairmen can control the use of the microphones they can make it quite hard for oppositional shareholders to be heard. In the event of a company proving unduly obstructive, one solution is for shareholder activists to try and smuggle their own amplification equipment into the meeting. However companies will usually try and prevent this. Company meetings often have elaborate 'security' precautions, involving airport-style metal detectors and hand-luggage X-ray machines. But these are not foolproof. Recently Greenpeace managed to get their voice heard at the 1991 ICI AGM, when three activists smuggled in briefcases with tape recorders, amplifiers and speakers hidden inside them. The briefcases were then activated to play messages about ICI's continuing production of ozone depleting chemicals.

Chapter 9
Informal Shareholder Action

The formal tools available to shareholders are reasonably flex-ible and effective as long as the shareholders concerned own a very large number of shares and have an organisation that it is able to devote large amounts time and money to dealing with shareholder action. For most shareholders, the con-straints on applying the formal tools are oppressive. Most shareholders have no real chance of using the standard pro-cedures to affect the policy of companies in the way the law intends. Fortunately there are a number of non-standard ways of using legal procedures, and of supplementing them with in-formal pressure activities. This chapter outlines some of these tactics, and covers some other issues relevant to taking share-holder action.

Pre-AGM Preparation

The AGM is commonly the biggest event of the year both for the company and for shareholder activists. The company will go to considerable lengths to prepare for the AGM so that it presents the right image to the shareholders and the City community. Shareholders activists should do the same. PAR-TiZANS, a shareholder action group dedicated to improving the policies of The RTZ Corporation PLC, prepare for the RTZ AGM by holding a day-long seminar a couple of months before the estimated date of the AGM. The purpose of the seminar is to familiarise those attending with the activities of RTZ and its subsidiaries, and to discuss PARTiZANS' strategy at the meeting. PARTiZANS invites various individuals and representatives of groups with special knowledge of RTZ's global operations to present detailed reports. After the report-ing is over the seminar discusses which issues it will focus on at the AGM; what questions should be asked; what press ac-tivities should be engaged in; what other briefing material is needed and who should prepare it; and whether to invite someone with personal experience of RTZ's operations from abroad. It also discusses practical issues including whether any of those present need shares or proxy nominations in order to attend the AGM; and where and when to hold a further meeting before the AGM to prepare detailed tactics and to allocate specific tasks at the AGM to specific people. Then, in the interim, a core of experienced PARTiZANS campaigners prepare questions for the meeting, buy and allocate RTZ shares and proxies, and prepare briefing material for the press and for other RTZ shareholders.

Gaining Admission to Meetings

Normally AGMs are limited just to directors, shareholders, their proxies and members of the press. To enforce this, the AGMs of large companies generally have some sort of security system for admissions to the meeting. Shareholders are sent forms that allow them admission to the meeting, or to appoint a proxy to attend the meeting in their place. There are three ways of gaining admission to meetings. Either by procuring admission forms, or by negotiating with the company to allow special admission, or by attempting to evade the security system. There are three ways to procure admission forms: by owning shares, by proxy nomination, or by 'borrowing' a shareholders' admission form. The latter is somewhat fraudulent as it involves passing oneself off as the shareholder whose name is on the admission form. However, while the security system can be rigorous, it will not require independent identification (like a passport), so it is easy to pretend to be another shareholder. This chicanery is not advisable as it is quite straightforward to buy shares, or to arrange for a shareholder to appoint a proxy (see page 133).

Using the proxy system has another advantage. The law allows shareholders who have appointed proxies to change their mind and attend the meeting themselves. If they do this they do not have to cancel their proxy nomination. If a shareholder and a proxy attend a meeting, only the shareholder's vote counts. While both votes do not count, however, both shareholder and proxy would seem to be able to attend the meeting. So one way to gain entry for additional people is for shareholders to appoint proxies to attend the meeting in their place, but to attend the meeting themselves anyway. If shareholder activists have a cooperative relationship with the company it may be possible to get it to agree to grant a concession to bring in extra people, particularly if the people for whom admission is required are 'respectable'. In one fairly exceptional situation anti-apartheid campaigners managed to negotiate an agreement with Shell to allow some non-shareholders into the meeting.

Regional Shareholders' Meetings

Many large companies, with huge numbers of shareholders dispersed throughout Britain, have adopted the practice of holding a few regional shareholder meetings. These are largely shareholder relations exercises, rather than the forum for shareholders to exercise their legal powers. However they may well be newsworthy events in the regional cities in which they are held, so they may be worth attending to get local press attention, and to communicate directly with the many shareholders who attend.

Briefing Materials

AGMs are a good place to distribute information to the target groups of a shareholder action campaign. Primarily, briefing materials tend to be aimed at the shareholders and the press. The briefing materials usually produced by shareholder activists take the form of a leaflet or a sheet of A4, stating the policy change desired of the company, the background to this policy change, details of the shareholder action group concerned and of its supporters, as well as details about how shareholders can get in contact with the action group. In order to get a better response from shareholders, some activist groups include a tear-off slip on the leaflet, inviting shareholders to return it, with their name and address, so they can be added to the mailing list to receive further information. It is worth having people available at the end of the meeting to collect these slips.

Briefing leaflets can be distributed to shareholders either outside the meeting as they come in, or inside the meeting. Many shareholders will arrive at the meeting early, so they will be sitting waiting with little to do, and so could well read leaflets that are handed to them.

Most actions at AGMs are not simply aimed at the directors and the shareholders, but at the press. Shareholder activist groups commonly issue a press release prior to the AGM, telling journalists what they are going to do and why. A company's AGM is the time in the year when the press, particularly the financial press, gives extra press coverage to each company. It is therefore a good time to try and organise press coverage. In addition to the press release, it is worth having a press statement ready to hand out to any journalists who become interested as a result of the meeting.

Shadow Reports

The most sophisticated approach to briefing materials that has been employed in Britain, is to produce a 'shadow annual report'. The End Loans to South Africa Campaign (ELTSA) produced several shadow annual reports for Barclays and Shell during the 1980s. These reports were well presented documents running to some twenty pages. The shadow reports were produced on behalf of 'shadow boards of directors'. The 1986 Barclays' shadow board included three academics; two union leaders; two members of parliament — including Neil Kinnock; Julie Christie, the actor; a campaigner; and local councillor; an ANC representative; and Donald Woods, the exiled South African newspaper editor made famous by the film *Cry Freedom*. ELTSA's shadow reports did not attempt to cover all aspects of company business, but instead focused on the issues relating to the continued involvement of Barclays and Shell in the apartheid system. The shadow reports constituted a considerable investment of time and money, but they created a very powerful impression of a heavy-weight campaign. In some years the shadow report and the meeting of the shadow board got more press coverage than Barclays' own AGM.

Debates and Statements

In addition to asking questions and putting resolutions to AGMs, shareholder activists have successfully arranged with the company to have time allocated at the AGM for a debate on their specific issue. There are several reasons why a company might be persuaded to agree to such an arrangement. Companies may allocate time specifically to shareholder activists in an attempt to contain discussion of controversial issues, preventing disruption of the rest of the meeting.

Disruption at an AGM tends not to reflect well on the company, so many companies would rather avoid it. If shareholders are disruptive one year, the company may be prepared to make some sort of concession to prevent disruption of the following year's meeting. One example of a concession of this kind took place at the 1990 Shell AGM. After disruption at previous meetings concerning Shell's involvement in South Africa, Shell came to an agreement with anti-apartheid campaigners, to set aside thirty minutes of the AGM purely for debating South African issues. Three anti-apartheid speakers were allowed seven minutes each to address the meeting, and then Shell's chairman spoke in the company's defence. The result of this was that the South Africa debate got a whole article to itself in *The Guardian*, when disruption would have perhaps generated a paragraph or two in the main article about the AGM. Whether shareholders have been disruptive in the past or not, it is worth pursuing the idea of trying to get companies to agree to allocate special time to a debate about activists' concerns. It is, after all, a way in which the company can demonstrate publicly what an open and democratic institution it is. If the company is not cooperative, threatening to try and bring a resolution to the AGM, while hinting that debating time would do just as well, might be persuasive. The fact that the company is prepared to allow formal space to discuss issues of concern, may not directly achieve any more than would have been won by ordinary questions, but, indirectly, a formal debate is a major achievement, because it shows the world that the company takes the issues seriously. Alternatively, rather than a full debate, a more modest request can be made of the company to give their permission for an group to make a formal statement of its concerns and criticisms.

Presentation of
Shareholder Action

Presentation is as important as content. The style of presentation depends on the particular objectives the shareholder campaign has for the AGM. If the purpose of action at the meeting is to get press attention, the presentation of the case and the kinds of shareholder action entered into will not be the same as that employed when the objective is to win the support of institutional shareholders.

One way that has been used increase the impact of shareholder presentations is to invite an influential figure to propose the resolution on the shareholder activists' behalf. In 1984 a coalition of anti-apartheid groups arranged for Archbishop Trevor Huddleston, the President of the Anti-Apartheid Movement, to propose their resolution to the Shell AGM to get it to disclose the amount of crude oil it was exporting to South Africa, and to stop the supply of refined oil. Alternatively, some shareholder action groups have invited people with first-hand personal experience of the relevant issues to attend. In 1991 Minewatch, a global coalition of groups campaigning on mining issues, invited four Navajo indians to the Hanson PLC AGM, to complain about its coal mining operations on their land. PARTiZANS has invited Australian aborigines and people from the Philippines to RTZ AGMs, as well as local British people who are affected by the operations of the company.

Disruption Inside the AGM

Sometimes it may be necessary to use more disruptive tactics in the AGM, for example heckling, singing and banner waving. This of course will not be popular with the company. If shareholder activists still have a fairly cooperative relationship with their company, seriously disruptive activity will probably be counterproductive. However if the relationship has broken down, or no progress is being made, there may be little choice but to take disruptive action. It is important to stage disruption carefully and sensitively. Heckling loudly from the beginning of the meeting and continuing throughout is more likely to be merely irritating than adding anything of positive value. Carefully planned disruption can be very useful and positive. For a start it wakes everybody up, including the press, and demonstrates that people are seriously concerned. Heckling works best if it is tied closely to inadequate or evasive responses from the chairman, rather than being hurled randomly. It is also an idea to slowly build up the tension, rather than shouting angrily before the meeting has warmed up. In this way shareholders can succeed in dramatically increasing the suspense at the meeting, and, more importantly, their disruptive behaviour can appear to be justified anger, genuinely tied to specific failures on behalf of the company, rather than fanatical ranting.

For example, at the 1992 RTZ AGM, shareholder activists produced what they alleged to be a leaked company report criticising the safety procedures of one of its subsidiaries' Namibian uranium mining operations. A PARTiZANS questioner challenged the chairman to either confirm or deny that the report had indeed been produced by the company. The chairman hedged. The dissident shareholders had been fairly quiet up to this point, but they then started shouting 'Answer the question, yes or no! Yes or No!' The chairman managed to avoid answering the question, but the heckling made his evasion abundantly clear. Furthermore this incident was reported in the press as arguably the most significant part of the meeting. If disruption is not carefully controlled it can appear aggressive and negative, losing the sympathy of a lot of the people whose support may be needed.

At an earlier RTZ AGM in 1982, some shareholders took disruptive action further. After a particularly demanding batch of questions, Sir Alastair Frame, then the chairman, decided to declare the meeting closed. There were however still many people wanting to ask questions. Some of whom started demanding an opportunity to speak. The chairman did not allow them to, and the directors prepared to leave the podium. In response, about 30 shareholder activists marched toward the front of the hall and climbed on to the podium and started to shout at the departing directors. The police were called by the stewards to help them remove the dissident shareholders, some of whom sat on the floor and had to be carried out. This attracted considerable publicity, with some coverage of the background issues that were provoking the shareholder action.

Much disruption takes place under the impulse of moral outrage. This can be effective as long as a the cause of the outrage is clear for all to see, so it does not appear as simple belligerence. The point of disruptive action however is not simply to vent anger, but to achieve a particular objective, so it is usually preferable to take disruptive action on the basis of a pre-meditated plan. This allows disruption to be imaginative, humorous and theatrical, rather than aggressive, and this can give it a better chance of being reported.

Groups in America have tried tactics like standing silently on their chairs in the meeting holding placards, offering prayers that the company improves its ways instead of asking questions, and producing physical evidence of the companies' activities. The Truro-based group Surfers Against Sewage (SAS) brought a plastic bag full of sewage related debris to the

1990 South West Water AGM. The bag included condoms and sanitary towels found washed up on the beaches in the South West Water region. As a result SAS stole the show.

Demonstrating Outside the AGM

There is more time and space outside the meeting hall to organise a demonstration or a press stunt, to get publicity and to get the attention of shareholders. Demonstrations, while not actually disrupting the process of the meeting, can be counterproductive for the same kind of reasons. They might inform shareholders about the issues, but they can all too easily alienate them. If demonstrations aim to get press coverage, then three questions worth considering are: what is so special about this demonstration that it will get press attention? Does it get the message across? Has the press been told about it? Demonstrations are not always reliable methods of securing press attention. Demonstrations occur all the time, so a demonstration has to be particularly interesting for it to get press coverage. One way of achieving this is by finding a hook to hang the story of on.

In 1988 Minorco launched a takeover bid for Consolidated Gold Fields. The financial press were producing dozens of column-inches of news-print on the takeover battle. It was a 'live' story. But there was more demand for stories than there was new information, so journalists were casting around for a new angle. Consolidated Gold Fields had operations in South Africa, so End Loans to South Africa used the takeover battle as a hook for some publicity. The activists organised a fake boxing match in order to humorously represent the takeover fight. In the match one boxer had the Minorco chairman's name written on him, and wore a cardboard mask with the chairman's face on it; the other did the same for the Consolidated Gold Fields chairman. Ringing the boxing match were lots of people holding clearly written banners criticising Consolidated Gold Fields's involvement in South Africa. From the press's point of view, this was a new angle on the takeover, and so the story and a photograph of the boxing match got into the papers, with the anti-apartheid banners in full view.

Good campaigners are always on the look-out for hooks to get press coverage. Another example of a successful press stunt came during a Friends of the Earth campaign to persuade the drinks company, Schweppes, to produce returnable bottles. In this case, Friends of the Earth campaigners collected thousands of Schweppes bottles and dumped them on the doorstep of the Schweppes offices.

Surfers Against Sewage is an excellent example of how a small imaginative group can gain press coverage. SAS was formed in 1990 by a few surfers objecting to the raw sewage released by South West Water into the sea off Cornwall. In the last two years, SAS has been the subject of a half-hour documentary on Channel 4, numerous BBC and ITV news items, a three page feature in the Mail on Sunday *You* magazine, and has been featured in articles in *The Times*, *The Daily Telegraph* and *The Mirror*. Admittedly there are few campaigns that can be represented as photogenically as those of SAS: a youthful surfer, riding the crest of a wave wearing a gas mask! SAS has had to work hard at persuading the media to run its stories. Its stunts include lobbying the House of Commons wearing wet suits, flippers and snorkels, a crawl to Southern Waters' head office (begging for cleaner seas), and a giant inflatable turd which is floated around Britain's coasts for local newspapers to take pictures of.

When performing press stunts, it is vital that the press is informed well in advance. Clearly worded banners or placards, with the group's name on, should be abundantly visible at the demonstration. Placards should aim to be communicative, and if possible humorous rather than abusive or overly-subtle. Alternatively, the style of the demonstration should clearly get the message across. Greenpeace activists, for example, regularly dress up in chemical protection suits when demonstrating about toxic waste. Outside the 1992 ICI AGM, 80 activists wearing protective white suits, sun glasses and sun-cream, sat down on the street holding placards saying 'ICI World Class Ozone Destroyers' (ICI had recently run an advertising campaign proclaiming that it was a 'world class company'). It is also important to have somebody on hand who is well briefed to act as a spokesperson, who can deal with any questions from the press, the public, the company, or the police.

Greenpeace has a reputation for being adept at press stunts. It is famous for imaginative, daring, and generally successful attempts to get publicity. It is noteworthy that Greenpeace's stunts are always very visual and often closely tied to the problem concerned. For example, Greenpeace activists regularly tie banners protesting against toxic pollution to the factory chimneys that they believe to be responsible for the pollution, or drive inflatable boats between the harpoon of a whaler and the hunted whale, putting their lives on the line.

Few shareholder activists may anticipate that they will act at the same level as Greenpeace, but the principles are the same.

There is a thin line between activities that aim to attract press coverage and 'direct action' which aims to intervene directly in the company's activities. Direct action involves some physical display of opposition to, or obstruction of, the company's operations — such as blocking access to a planned development site by lying in the middle of the road. Non-violent direct action has been famously effective in the past for bringing independence to India and civil rights to America. If it is bold, disciplined and carefully planned, direct action can generate a powerful moral platform on which to base more mundane action. But it has its disadvantages: it can be costly in personal terms; it can easily go wrong, and in as much as it gives shareholder activists the moral high ground it can make the company's activities look morally reprehensible, leading it to adopt an uncooperative and defensive posture. Direct action should be related as closely as possible to the issues it is concerned with, so that message is clear; it should aim to enlist the sympathy of people rather than alienate them, and it should be within at least the spirit of the law.

After the AGM

After the AGM, in order to assess the success or failure at achieving campaign objectives and to learn from any mistakes, it is worth holding a debriefing meeting with the members of the action group who attended. It is probably worth writing up an account of the AGM for the group's own records, this process is also useful basis for a post-AGM report which can be sent out to supporters and the press, indicating what future action is planned and what the supporters can do to follow up the action at the AGM. Another post-AGM exercise is for the group to write to its contacts in the company giving an assessment of the AGM, responding to any points that the directors made at the meeting, and restating the group's position in the light of any developments arising from the meeting.

In Britain there is no legal requirement for companies to send shareholders minutes or reports of the proceedings of the annual general meeting. This is unfortunate because it means that the majority of shareholders (who were not at the AGM) never find out in detail what took place. However the law does require companies to keep minutes of the annual general meeting, and shareholders do have a right to see these minutes. They are available from the company secretary's office.

Conclusion

In the USA, shareholder action is becoming a standard part of company and shareholder life. Several hundred social responsibility and corporate governance resolutions are filed by oppositional shareholders each year, up from virtually none two decades ago. Corporate policy has changed remarkably in a number of areas, due substantially to the dialogue, negotiation and pressure orchestrated by American shareholder activists.

The American shareholder culture is beginning to cross the atlantic. Both directly, in the form of US institutional investors who hold shares in British companies; and indirectly, as ideas, strategies, and institutions developed in the USA are replicated in this country.

There is a long way to go before shareholder activism becomes standard practice in Britain. Ultimately it will not happen until the mainstream financial community — pension funds, insurance companies, local authorities, church funds, stockbrokers, and unit trusts — recognise the important role active shareholders can play in British business. The more individuals and groups of private citizens are prepared to take carefully planned, intelligent shareholder action, the more quickly this day will come.

Appendix A
Bibliography

A Basic PR Guide Dorothy and Alastair MacIntosh (Directory of Social Change, 1985)

Best Companies for Women Scarlett MccGwire (Pandora, 1992)

The Better World Investment Guide Moira Alperson *et al* (Prentice Hall, New York, 1991)

Britain's Best Employers? Sean Hamil (Kogan Page, 1993)

Butterworth's Company Law Handbook 7th edition ed. Keith Walmsley (Butterworth, 1990) (contains current Companies Acts)

Butterworth's Company Law Guide 2nd edition, eds. Michael Renshall and Keith Walmsley (Butterworth, 1990) (contains detailed exposition of the Companies Acts)

The Campaigning Handbook Mark Lattimer (Directory of Social Change, 1993)

Changing Corporate Values Richard Adams *et al* (Kogan Page, 1991)

Controlling Companies Geoffrey Mills (Unwin, 1988)

Corporate Citizen magazine (Directory of Social Change, quarterly)

Corporate Social Reporting R. Gray *et al* (Prentice-Hall, 1987)

The Directory of Directors (Thomas Skinner, annually)

Directory of Grant Making Trusts (Charities Aid Foundation, 1991)

Environmental Grants (Directory of Social Change, 1993)

Ethical Consumer (ECRA Publishing, quarterly)

Ethical Investor, The (EIRIS, quarterly)

Extel Cards (Extel Statistical Services, 37 Paul Street, London EC2A 4PB; available at larger libraries)

The Global Consumer Phil Wells and Mandy Jetter (Gollancz, 1991)

Green Reporting Dave Owen, ed. (Chapman Hall, 1992)

A Guide to the Major Trusts 3rd edition, Luke FitzHerbert and Michael Eastwood, eds. (Directory of Social Change, 1991)

The Hambro Company Guide (Hemmington Scott, quarterly)

Introduction to Company Law L.H. Leigh *et al* (Butterworth, 1987)

McCarthy Cards (McCarthy's Information Services, Manor House, Ash Walk, Warminster; available at larger libraries)

The Principles of Modern Company Law 5th edition, L.C.B. Gower *et al* (Stevens, 1979)

Pressure: The A to Z of Campaigning in Britain Des Wilson (Heinemann, 1984)

Raising Money from Trusts Michael Norton (Directory of Social Change, 1992)

The Shareholder Simon Rose (Mercury Books, 1991)

Socially Responsible Investment 2nd edition, Sue Ward (Directory of Social Change, 1991)

Who Owns Whom (Dun & Bradstreet, annually)

Using the Media Denis MacShane (Pluto Press, 1979)

Appendix B
Addresses of Organisations

Below is a list of contact addresses of organisations involved in action on companies, or able to provide information on companies and on social and environmental issues.

Amnesty International (British Section), 99-119 Rosebery Avenue, London EC1R 4RE

Anti-Apartheid Movement, 13 Mandela Street, London NW1 0DW

British Union for the Abolition of Vivisection (BUAV), 16A Crane Grove, London N7 8LB

Business in the Community, 227A City Road, London EC1V 1LX

Business in the Environment, 41 Threadneedle Street, London EC2R 8AP

CND, 162 Holloway Road, London N7 8DQ

Campaign Against Arms Trade (CAAT), 11 Goodwin Street, Finsbury Park, London N4 3HQ

Campaign for Freedom of Information, 88 Old Street, London EC1V 9AR

Catholic Fund for Overseas Development (CAFOD), 2 Romero Close, Stockwell Road, London SW19 9TY

Charities Aid Foundation, 48 Pembury Road, Tonbridge, Kent TN9 2JD

Christian Aid, P O Box 100, London SW1 7RT

Church Commissioners, 1 Millbank, London SW1P 3JZ

Christian Ethical Investment Group, 90 Booker Avenue, Bradwell Common, Milton Keynes MK13 8EF

Commission for Racial Equality (CRE), Elliot House, 10-12 Allington Street, London SW1E 5EH

Companies House, Cardiff CF4 3UZ

Compassion in World Farming, 20 Lavant Street, Petersfield, Hampshire GU32 3EW

Confederation of British Industry (CBI), Centre Point, New Oxford Street, London WC1A 1GU

Council for Economic Priorities (CEP), 30 Irving Place, New York 10003-2366, USA

Ecumenical Committee for Corporate Responsibility (ECCR), 11 Burnham Wood, Fareham PO16 7UD

Ethical Investment Research Service Ltd (EIRIS), 504 Bondway Business Centre, 71 Bondway, London SW8 1SQ

End Loans to South Africa (ELTSA), c/o Methodist Church, 56 Camberwell Road, London SE5 0EN

Equal Opportunities Commission (EOC), Head Office, Overseas House, Quay Street, Manchester M3 3HN

Friends of the Earth (FoE), 26-28 Underwood Street, London N1 7JQ

Fund for the Replacement of Animals in Medical Experiments (FRAME), Eastgate House, 34 Stoney Street, Nottingham NG1 1NB

Greenpeace, Canonbury Villas, London N1 2PN

Her Majesty's Inspectorate of Pollution (HMIP), Romney House, 43 Marsham Street, London SW1P 3PY

Industrial Society, 3 Carlton House Terrace, London SW1Y 5DG

Institute of Personnel Management, IPM House, 35 Camp Road, Wimbledon, London SW19 4UX

Interfaith Center for Corporate Responsibility (ICCR), Room 566, 475 Riverside Drive, New York NY 10115-0050, USA

Jupiter Tarbutt Merlin, Knightsbridge House, 197 Knightsbridge, London SW7 1RB

Keep Sunday Special, Jubilee House, 3 Hooper Street, Cambridge CB1 2NZ

Labour Research Department (LRD), 78 Blackfriars Road, London SE1 8HF

National Council for Voluntary Organisations (NCVO), 26 Bedford Square, London WC1B 3HU

National Rivers Authority (NRA), 30-34 Albert Embankment, London SE1 7TL

New Economics Foundation (NEF), 2nd Floor, Universal House, 88-94 Wentworth Street, London E1 7SA

OXFAM, 274 Banbury Road, Oxford, Oxfordshire OX2 7DZ

PARTiZANS, 210 Liverpool Road, London N1 1LE

Pensions Investment Research Consultants (PIRC), Challoner House, 19-21 Clerkenwell Close, London EC1R 0AA

Public Interest Research Centre Ltd, Box 111, London NW1 8XG

The Share Centre Ltd, PO Box 1000, Tring, Herts HP23 4JR

Scottish Arts Legal Fund, Two/Left, 64 White Street, Glasgow G11 5EB

Surfers Against Sewage, The Old Counthouse Warehouse, Wheal Kitty, St Agnes, Truro, Cornwall TR5 0RE

SustainAbility, 91-97 Freston Road, London W11 4BD

Taskforce on the Churches and Corporate Responsibility (TCCR), 129 St Clair Avenue West, Toronto, Ontario, Canada M4V 1N5

TUC, Press Office, Great Russell Street, London WC1B 3LS

Traidcraft, Kingsway, Gateshead, Tyne and Wear NE11 0NE

UK Social Investment Forum, Keely House, 22-30 Keely Road, Croydon CR0 1TE

United Kingdom Shareholders Association, Half Tiles, Roseacre Gardens, Chilworth, near Guildford, Surrey GU4 8RQ

United Nations Association, 3 Whitehall Court, London SW1A 2EL

United Shareholders Association (USA), 1667 K Street NW, Suite 770, Washington DC 20006, USA

Women's Environmental Network (WEN), 287 City Road, London EC1V 1LA

World Development Movement (WDM), 25 Beehive Place, Brixton, London SW9 7QR

World Wide Fund for Nature (WWF), Panda House, Weyside Park, Godalming, Surrey GU7 1XR

Notes

1. Tawney, R.H, *Religion and the Rise of Capitalism*, Holland Memorial Lectures, 1922 (Pelican, 1938)

2. Leigh, L.H. *et al, Introduction to Company Law* (Butterworth, 1987) p.2

3. Leigh, L.H. *et al*, p.2

4. Goyder, G. *The Just Enterprise* (André Deutsch, 1987).

5. See Tricker, R.I. *Corporate Governance* (Gower, 1984) p.34

6. Gower, L.C.B *Modern Company Law*, 3rd edition (Stevens, 1969) p.49

7. Tricker, R.I. *op cit*, p.36

8. *Government Command Paper* 6659 para 5 (HMSO, 1945)

9. Gower, *ibid*, p.56

10. Jay, President of the Board of Trade, 1967, House of Commons Debates, Vol 741, col. 359

11. Leigh. L.H. *et al, op cit*

12. Lord Haldane, House of Lords, 1915, quoted in Gower, *op cit*, p.145. Italics added

13. Gower, *op cit*, p.147

14. Quoted by Gower, *ibid*, p.149

15. See Appendix A

16. Companies Act 1985, S309

17. Gower, *op cit*, p.522

18. Gower, *ibid*, p.130

19. Lord Justice Evershed, Short *v.* Treasury Commissioners 1948 (Gower, *ibid*)

20. *Cadbury Committee on the Financial Aspects of Corporate Governance Draft Report*, 1992, p.34 (italics added)

21. *Financial Times*, 30.7.92

22. Companies Act 1985, S309.

23. *Cadbury Report, op cit,* para 2.2

24. *Cadbury Report, ibid,* paragraph 5.3.

25. Alastair Blair, *Financial Times* 27.5.92

26. Alastair Blair, *ibid*

27. *Cadbury Report, ibid,* paragraph 3.4

28. *Cadbury Report, ibid,* paragraph 6.3

29. For a discussion of the question of whether it is more appropriate to consider shareholders' responsibilities as those of owners or those of members of an association, see page 43

30. *Cadbury Report, op cit,* paragraph 6.4

31. *Cadbury Report, ibid,* paragraph 6.2

32. PIRC Intelligence, July/August 1992.

33. *Cadbury Report, op cit,* paragraph 4.9

34. *Cadbury Report, ibid,* paragraph 4.8

35. *Cadbury Report, ibid,* paragraph 1.8

36. Command Paper 6707 (HMSO, 1977)

37. Gower, *ibid,* p.69.n

38. PIRC Intelligence, July/August 1992, p.8

39. PIRC Intelligence, July/August 1992, p.9

40. Wilson. D, *Pressure: The A-Z of Campaigning in Britain* (Heinemann Educational, 1984) p.28

41. Wilson, D, *ibid,* p.30

42. Wilson, D, *ibid,* p.30

43. Wilson, D, *ibid,* p.30

44. Wilson, D, *ibid,* p.36

45. Stock Exchange Yellow Book, 1.07 para 4

46. See the Race Equality and Employment Project (REEP), Interim Report (The Ecumenical Committee for Corporate Responsibility, 1992).

47. Wilson, D, *op cit,* p.53

48. Jill McWilliam MBE, Public Relations Director, Iceland Frozen Foods PLC

49. Wilson, D, *op cit,* p.56-57

50. Anne Simpson, Joint Managing Director, PIRC. Speech to the 1991 PIRC corporate governance conference

51. *The Economist*, 7.9.91

52. *The Economist*, 30.5.92

53. Examples are the South Shore Bank in the USA and Shared Interest in the UK

54. For more information see Denis McShane, *Using the Media* (Pluto Press, 1979)

55. Elizabeth Holtzman, comptroller of New York, at 1991 PIRC conference on 'Pension Funds and Corporate Governance'.

56. Companies Act 1985, S379

57. Companies Act 1985, S377

58. See Appendix B for details about Companies House

59. Companies Act 1985, S376, paragraph 5

60. The motion was proposed by the Project on Corporate Responsibility, and is quoted in Alperson, M, *et al*, *The Better World Investment Guide* (Prentice Hall, New York, 1991), p.5

61. *The Better World Investment Guide*, *ibid*

62. Companies Act 1985, S303

63. Gower, *op cit*, p.349

64. Gower, *ibid*, p.492

65. Companies Regulations 1985, Table A paragraph 51

Index